Room in the Heart

SURVIVING A CHILDHOOD UNDONE, FULFILLING A PACT TO LOVE

Dana Andrews

I believe *wishes* can be hugs of hope. I dedicate this book to you, the reader, with a heart that understands your hurt and embraces your healing.

With warmest wishes, Dana

A Note from the Editor

The very first time I talked to Dana, I knew she was onto something big. Just hearing her passion for spreading love to others made me want to be a part of what she was doing. After I read her manuscript, I knew for sure that her work *had* to be published so that survivors like Dana could take heart from her journey and share her message of healing, resilience, and peace.

Though I'm not a survivor of abuse, Dana's work impacted me as a mother, daughter, sister, wife, and friend. It made me think of loved ones who have been through hellish times in their lives—like periods of crushing clinical depression—and feel greater empathy and compassion for their struggles. It's easy to pay lip service to supporting people in need, but it's far more difficult to meet them where they are, listen without offering judgment, and show them kindness with an open heart.

Even if you, like me, are not personally a victim of abuse, you may have your own painful history to overcome. Dana's story has far-reaching applications for every human life. When it comes down to it, we all want the same thing: to fill our lives with as much light and love as possible.

If, however, you have experienced or are currently experiencing abusive relationships, Dana's story may speak to you in a special way. Study after study shows a clear connection between abuse, low self-worth, depression, and, tragically, suicide.

This book can literally save lives by reaching people who feel empty and alone and motivating *all* of us to help one another—and help ourselves as well. Thanks to Dana's online community, which you can connect with at iamdanaandrews.com and facebook.com/iamdanaandrews, we can reach one another and spread the love with the click of a button. When we work together and ask our friends for help, we can do great things!

Room in the Heart is Dana's story, but in some ways, it belongs to all of us. I hope you enjoy reading it as much as I did!

Elizabeth Watson
Editor

Acknowledgments

There are so many things that have led me to write this book, but in all honesty, it is the sweet souls who have entered both my life and my heart, who entirely made this possible. The man I met when I was only fifteen, and who would become my beautiful and incredibly loving husband, has loved me more than I will ever understand. You gave me a role I could not cherish more, and five beautiful children who are truly making a difference in the world. If not for this beautiful family, I would have had nothing to write. For your love, understanding, and laughter, I am unequivocally grateful. You are my every reason, and are the song my heart sings with each gift of a new day…

There are those who walk through life doing what they do best, but sadly, never have the chance to know of the impact they made on others' souls. For me, that will never be the case. It is my passion to always love with a full heart, and to take nothing and no one for granted. My dear friends Louisa Latela, Marilyn Hajer, and Diane Hayden Dufford, who believed in me all along, and carried my soul through times when burdens seemed too big to bear: you each held my hands across the miles and through the years. This is why I am still here—my husband and children cannot thank you enough for that! My sweet fairy godmother, Joan Ianieri, taught me the art of unconditional loving. I always knew that when I climbed up your front porch steps, both your front door and your heart would welcome me in. When I felt fatally flawed and unworthy of anyone's love, you hugged me, you listened to me, and you were your wonderful self! You had an immeasurable impact upon the mother I am. My family and I can never possibly thank you enough. I will forever hold you close to my soul. When I felt it was finally the right time to get this memoir published, a beautiful angel took me beneath her splendid wings, and understood my need to place it into the hands of all who need hope. Elizabeth Watson, you have become my partner-in-crime, stopping at nothing to bring this book to fruition. May you always share my appreciation for the gifts and opportunities we have been given. I believe this memoir qualifies as both paying it forward and making a huge difference. Also, to my friend Miriam Seidel: Thank you for your editing expertise and for your support in encouraging me to write every day.

I would be incredibly remiss if I were not to thank Louis Greenstein for coming into my life and making this book possible by feeding my hungry soul with such hope. You are the obstetrician who delivered my sixth child. For your kindness, time, talent, and humility, I offer a "thank you" that comes from a hugely indebted heart. Now you can walk through your life knowing what you do best—I refer not only to your brilliant writing, but the generous giving of your soul. It is my hope that your giving will go well beyond my efforts—all the way to the souls of this book's readers. May you always feel the depth of my gratitude upon your heart…

CHAPTER 1

The Pact

"Since you were a mistake, we were planning to abort you."

I vividly remember hearing my mother say these words to me, in a cool, matter-of-fact tone. I was about six years old, sitting in the back seat of our family car, my baby brother Lawrence beside me. I listened, frozen in my seat, as my mother went on:

"Then we realized that you might be the boy we dreamed we might some-day have. Didn't you ever wonder why you and Bianca are only thirteen months apart? Your father and I tried for almost a year to get pregnant with her. When she was only four months old, I accidentally got pregnant with you. Bianca was so adorable and funny, and we were so happy with her—how could any other baby even compare? Well, unless it was a boy, of course." Of all the things I did wonder, that was certainly not one of them.

From the front seat, my older sister, Bianca, turned her head towards me and delivered a sickening, self-assured grin. It was a given that only she belonged in the front seat next to our mother; I was always reminded that Bianca came first, and it was she who deserved first choice on everything from clothes, to outings, to sitting in the front seat.

Our mother often reminisced about these things, reminding us how smart and amazing Bianca was, and how when I was an infant, all of Mother's friends told her I was neither cute nor smart. I was not the chubby, gregarious first born who was planned and long awaited. I was the skinny, quiet one, content to suck my thumb and watch the world hammer on. I hardly cried, but even so, somehow made life inconvenient from the time I was mistakenly conceived, to my birth, when I was not, in fact, the boy they had wished for. To make matters worse, apparently I refused to nurse, making my mother engorged, forcing her to lie in bed with ice on her breasts. "Oh, the pain you caused me! I was not very happy with you," she would say.

"We thought you were retarded," Mother mused. "You just sucked your thumb and stared into space. My friends said, 'Look at how wonderful Bianca is! Dana doesn't matter. She's not even cute!'" In early infancy, I developed a cyst on my eyelid that had to be removed. Mother told me that she made my dad take me to the hospital "in case I died," because she didn't want to be there if that happened. When my dad brought me home later that night, mother recalled, "You smelled like the ether anesthetic they used. You stunk! I couldn't even get near you or hold you." My father told me how much he enjoyed holding me as an infant, I was so calm and content—but I had to be content with being held when he got home late each night.

As we became toddlers, Bianca was still chubby, with twinkly eyes that matched her outgoing, adored personality. I was skinny, seldom spoke, and had huge saucer-like eyes that, unbeknownst to mother and her friends, took everything in. Always I was placed on the back burner, forever held accountable for having been such an inconvenience from the start. I have a memory from the age of two, of being wildly spanked while on my changing table because I had dirtied my diaper. I was yanked out of my crib, half asleep, and made to feel so guilty and "bad." Mother was angrier still because she had to take off my shoes to bathe me. She refused to take off my shoes when she put me in my crib for naptime because removing my shoes was "inconvenient" for her.

From early on, I was made to feel unloved, flawed, and unmistakably a mistake. Neither my parents nor my siblings had any use for me, other than to mock and belittle me. Yet part of me held onto little scraps of hope. I wanted to believe that God planned for me to be here. If there were indeed a God, I would tell myself, I would amount to something after all. Something deep inside my soul whispered to me that I was born for some kind of real purpose. I had to look for it on the sly, as my attempts to find who I was were constantly swamped by my mother's behavior toward me. As a child, I dreamed of another kind of life: about one day having kids myself, and making a home where we had plentiful love, laughter, pets, and every reason to have little parties to celebrate anything happy.

I remember one particular night, when I was nine years old. That day my mother had reminded me once again that I was "a mistake that was to be aborted." As I lay in bed that night, I decided to make a pact with God. I promised that I would gladly accept as many children as He would give me, so that I could undo, as many times as possible, the childhood I had endured. Just thinking this filled me with hope. After this, my secret pact gave me an escape hatch from my painful present, allowing me to enter a future that held everything I wanted. I could imagine spreading my happiness not only to my children, but also beyond them. Certainly I was not the only one who ever had or would have an unhappy childhood. I would somehow find a way to bring happiness to the hearts of my children's friends who shared my childhood fate. No child I knew would cry him/herself to sleep if I could help it.

It would be many more years before I began to figure out what made my mother act the way she did towards me. Since she talked a lot about herself, I knew that my mother's birth was also unplanned. Neither of her two older brothers welcomed her with open arms. When she was young, her wealthy parents were hardly ever home, often taking long trips through Europe. While her parents were away, she and her brothers would be left to stay with her two eccentric aunts. Her brothers would tease her mercilessly, and they punished her by hiding her dolls. Mother had trouble learning to read, and she felt inferior to her brothers, who were much older than her, and both highly intelligent—one became a professor of philosophy, and the other a successful artist. This may be one reason she spent most of her adult life on a mission to impress others with her "intelligence." Unfortunately, the time she spent with her crazy aunts left her with no boundaries and with very odd thinking. These women were rude, nosey, dogmatic, and exceptionally arrogant.

I believe her madness and inappropriate behavior can be traced to this experience. She often acted immaturely, even bizarrely—to the point of others' embarrassment. She would often walk around the house naked after showering, even when Lawrence was in his early teen years. I somehow knew instinctively that this was both odd and inappropriate; but when I told her I was uncomfortable with it, she would look at her very overweight naked body in a full-length mirror and tell me her body was beautiful. She believed that she could and should do whatever she wanted, and anyone who got in her way would suffer the consequences.

Mother also loved to tell dirty jokes to people she hardly knew or just recently met—it was her way of sizing them up. Those with solid boundaries would object, thereby placing themselves on her "bad" list. "How *dare* they not want to listen to my jokes?" she would rant later. "They don't even know what they are missing. They are sick in the head and need help!" In later years, she even included these inappropriate jokes in emails to our children. If I objected, she insisted that it was her right, that I was being a prude, and that I had no sense of humor. Those who did laugh at her jokes and pathetic behavior became immediate friends. But she constantly had to replenish her supply of friends; any time anyone offered even the least hint of an objection, she took that as a total rejection, and she pushed them out. Then she would make sure to broadcast the details to anyone who would listen, using her latest enemy as an example of what awaited those who crossed her.

My mother never attended college; she became a phlebotomist and worked in a hospital, hoping she would find a doctor to marry. When she met my dad, he was practicing in general medicine. Even though he was much older than she was, my mother quickly took charge in their relationship. She pushed him into changing his field of practice to psychiatry, telling him that if he were in an area of medicine requiring house calls, she was afraid "some woman might steal him from her." That's right—my mother's behavior toward me took place even though our father was a psychiatrist, someone who should have been trained to recognize and handle toxic behavior. This was another mystery I couldn't confront until much later.

Mother's irrational jealousy toward other women continued after they got married. And it expanded to include me, her daughter. My dad had stopped hugging me after I was five or six. When I asked my mother once why he never hugged me like my friends' dads hugged them, she said, "That would be incestuous." She was the one who had discouraged him from touching me, out of her own twisted misunderstanding. Not only was I undeserving of love from anyone, but in her eyes, I was also perverted for even thinking it was normal to want to be hugged by my dad. Once again, I was taught to never expect to be loved, cherished, or even appreciated. After all, I wasn't even supposed to be alive...

Even though we were so close in age, Bianca never played with me; she would go out clothes shopping with my mother or play with her own friends. I was not welcome to have friends come over, and my mother was certainly not willing to take me anywhere, let alone to a friend's house, especially when I might need to be picked up. Occasionally a friend's mother would pick me up at our house and later bring me home, which was something I looked forward to. Once I got home, however, my mother would begin her interrogation. She would start by asking whether the friend's family was rich or poor, whether they had rugs and antiques in their house, and what her parents did for a living.

Then would come the dreaded, humiliating question: "Were you peeking at one another's vaginas?" *Why* did she always ask me that? I never did that—it wasn't anything I even thought of doing. It was so embarrassing and demeaning. I sensed, even if I couldn't explain it, that this was her own issue—and it wasn't ok for her to make it mine.

Yet this feared behavior was just one of many items on her list of "evil things to never ever do." I knew all too well that if I did something, even unintentionally, that crossed the line into prohibited behavior, I risked being the recipient of one of Mother's meltdowns. Generally it began with a loud, berating condemnation. Her emotional crumbling would progress to her crying and sobbing, "Look what you have done to me! Your sister and brother don't do these things to me. Just remember, you only have one mother!" (I took this to mean, "You are one of my three children, so you are dispensable. I am the only circus in town, while you are just one, apparently substandard, undesirable venue.")

The next step in this all-too-familiar process would involve her getting on the phone, in my presence, to call every friend who would answer her call, so she could tell them her version of what *I* had done *to her*. As she finished with these phone conversations, she would tell me, "Get out of my sight. I don't even want to look at you." Sometimes as I slunk away, already miserable, I would hear her say, "What a stupid bitch she is."

Then would come my sentence, imposed by a three-person tribunal. Mother sent me to my room and would not talk to me for at least two or three days. If I left my room, I made sure she couldn't see me. Bianca would stand by my door and report what she heard from inside my room, while fabricating stories that might enhance my punishment. The third person on the tribunal was my dad.

My father was hardly ever home while I was awake. He worked long hours, leaving for work early in the morning and coming home late at night. My mother didn't seem bothered by this; she was content with the perks of having the income of a doctor's wife: shopping for matching shoes and bags and having a house filled with fine furniture and antiques. She was also happy to use him as an ever-present threat for me. ("Just wait until your father comes home.") I remember one school night, when I made the mistake of questioning why I had to wear Bianca's worn shoes and huge hand-me-downs—my sister was still much bigger than me. Mother made me sit in my bed, while she pulled up a chair at the foot of the bed and screamed at me every time I began to fall sleep, still sitting up. Finally, my father came home at eleven p.m., and he appeased her by pulling down my pants and spanking me. Then I was finally allowed to fall asleep, albeit with tears in my eyes.

Until the age of ten, I was such a deep sleeper that I would wet my bed. Mother decided that this must stop, and she devised a way to accomplish this. Every night after my father came home, he would yank me out of a heavy slumber and throw me onto the toilet seat. If I did not pee right away, he would lift me up and spank me. I think he worked late partly to avoid having to be "the bad guy who had to spank me." Sadly, the child psychiatrist could not protect his own child from the cruel caricature of a mother who was his wife. With all his psychiatric training, he could not fix her. If he didn't go along with her, he risked becoming her next victim: being sentenced to her silent treatment and to public embarrassment and ridicule by her to her circle of friends. My father avoided confronting her, and chose not to protect me, because the repercussions simply weren't worth being exposed to her wrath. I was the mistake.

I wonder how many people may have guessed the nightmare I was living. To look at us, we were a family who were doing well, living in a good neighborhood. Our house was a well-manicured split-level with a pool in the backyard. Inside, it was a museum filled with antiques and fine oil paintings, many of which had belonged to my grandmother. They were arranged perfectly in rooms that I was not allowed to enter. My mother reminded us often that we were "rich," that we had "wall-to-wall rugs."

Our house was definitely not a home—it lacked what a home has: love and a feeling of belonging. How could I feel safe in a house with rooms that echoed with my mother's shrieking threats? No, I learned what a home was by looking elsewhere. My best friend Christine, whom I met in third grade, used to come and play at my house. She would tell me, "You are so lucky because you are rich." She didn't realize I wore my sister's ill-fitting hand-me-downs, and I got haircuts at the barber. I preferred going to her house; although her family's house was modest, it was filled with love. When I went to visit, her mother would always stop whatever she was doing to give me a hug and ask how I was. This woman really cared—and she probably sensed my great need for simple, unconditional affection. Looking back, I believe that had it not been for Joan Ianieri, I might have become a mother like my own. Every time I came over, she showed me so much love, concern, and acceptance. She actively listened to me and cared about what I had to say! And she had no hidden or confusing agendas, like my mother did. Christine's mother showed me what sweet mothering was.

My mother would tell me how lucky we were, compared to my friend's family: they were "poor," her dad was only a gardener, and they didn't even have any rugs in their house. My friend's mother didn't have a fur coat, drive a fancy car, go clothes shopping all the time, or have a cleaning lady like we did. My mother certainly did love all of her possessions. But I realized early on that we lived in a museum, while my friend lived in a home. She had parents who focused on living, not collecting. They were a family whose bedrock was their appreciation and concern for one another. I will never allow my heart to forget the palpable feeling of real love in that little "house without rugs." That sweet house, which felt like a huge hug each time I walked through their door... Years later, I called Joan to tell her that *she* is the one who first made me believe that mothers can be good. She gave me hope. I wanted her to know that the love she gave me continues on through me unto my children.

Through the years, as I was subjected to hurtful moments like these and many more, somehow I managed to piece together bits of hope and solace that kept me going. When I was stuck in my room for another infraction, I would lose myself in my drawing and painting and later in my music. I learned to imagine a safe place for myself, a place where I was loved and happy. I reached out to friends and kind adults.

And I never forgot my pact—the pact I made with God, lying in bed that night when I was nine years old: that I would accept as many children as God would give me, so I could undo my childhood as many times as possible and shower them with love. I would make sure they knew the feeling that was so absent in my childhood.

As my life unfolded through much heartache and many small miracles, I did not give up on that dream. I was blessed to meet and fall in love with Will, the wonderful, caring man I married. Together we greeted in turn our five beautiful children. Starting when they were small, I never forgot my vision: to feed our children a steady diet of love and encouragement, the opposite of the diet I had been given. Will and I chose to let our kids discover their interests, and we celebrated their creative efforts. Thanks to Will's developing career, we lived in a succession of houses, and they were all *homes*—very loud, appropriately messy, exuberant homes! I found a particular joy in being able to be my creative self with my kids: constructing an edible castle as a school project with our son Scott, with cookie-dough bricks and a candy-bar drawbridge; keeping all our kids well-supplied in art materials, especially the big crayon boxes I had wished for but never got as a child.

As the children were growing up, I would write a holiday letter, which went out to our family and to friends we gathered with every geographical move. It was a fun way for me to keep in touch, while also assimilating the changes in our family from year to year. Each letter brought comments from those receiving them, suggesting I become a writer in my next life—which made me laugh. My immediate goal was trying to keep up with ensuring my husband and kids had their lunches packed for the next day! It was enough of a challenge to find the time to write the letters and address the envelopes—although I did have many little helpers willing to lick stamps. Sixteen years after the first letter was written, with our youngest applying to colleges and writing essays, I was struck by the thought that these letters, taken together, are part of my own life's essay, each one revealing another chapter of my family's growth. They serve as reminders and lessons about love, loss, laughter, and hope.

In the process of putting them together, though, I realized that their meaning could only be fully revealed when seen against the shadow of my childhood experiences and my long struggle to be free of my mother's influence. Only then could someone else understand why, for me, those small family moments are such a cause for celebration and gratitude. It has not been easy for me to revisit the pain that was such a constant in my childhood and teen years—but now I feel I've set down both sides of the story, to share with you. It is my hope that you take whatever you can from what I've written, both dark and light. May these words conjure up your old memories, assist you in assimilating your own circumstances, and serve to sweeten your days to come.

December 1995

Merry Christmas, Happy Chanukah, and a very Happy New Year!

To me, the past five years have seemed more like Easter than anything else! To explain, we will have moved four times within the span of five years. I know that I always seem to be saying, "Things are always hopping at the Andrews household," but we are talking about three-thousand-mile hops!

Early this February we are planning to move to Massachusetts. We have found the closest thing to our dream house: a large, three-story Colonial Victorian home on fourteen acres, built in 1740. Fortunately, the previous owner was a builder who completely modernized and updated the essentials, while preserving the historic elements. There is the perfect spot for my spinning wheel by the ten-foot-long kitchen fireplace, along with a nook for bread baking, two barns, woods, and a creek in the back of the property. I finally get to enjoy the gazebo that I have always wished for. To say that we are all very enthusiastic about this new place we'll soon call home is an understatement. Old wooden floors, here we come!

There are several reasons for our relocation. Mainly, being transplanted East Coast folks, we really have missed the seasons that Northern California couldn't provide, but we especially missed the snow. We also missed our friends and family who live back east. Lastly, it was a total thrill for Will to be offered the chance to practice at the same institution where he received his medical training. Besides his full-time career in medicine, this busy guy is also a gentleman farmer—on our five acres we have three sheep, two turkeys, two ducks, one rooster and a dozen hens, plus our two dogs, India and Iman. Will is always happy to do whatever needs to be done to keep his family and farm happy!

Marching along, each to their own tune, are our five children. Scott, now ten years old, boasts a wonderful sense of humor. When feeding the sheep he talks to them, telling the lambs they are "bahhh-utiful" and the oldest sheep, "You are 'pasture' prime!" He spent the last year home schooling in order to satisfy his insatiable quest for knowledge. He can tell you everything about the Egyptian Pyramids, ancient history, cellular structure, and all types of pollution. This homeschooling has turned out to be a joint effort between Will and myself.

Eight-year-old Robert is one gregarious guy, and he continues to be exceedingly industrious and artistic. He is in third grade, and he has started a home business selling his illustrations with peoples' photographs superimposed. (Have you never seen a cartoon drawing of a chubby little diaper-clad baby with your picture as the face?) Robert's little antics often concern making light of others' names; he has renamed his loving Nana and Grandpop "Banana and Grandpopsicle." At dinnertime, he sings "Old MacDonald" with his sisters' and brothers' names substituted for animal names. Having five kids within eight years' time, I am simply too tired by that hour to protest.

Alexander will turn six in early February. Alexander is a sweet, sensitive, and especially cerebral little boy, who is currently fixated on the numbers "googol" and "infinity." When he started kindergarten this year, I introduced him to his teacher, but he insisted he was "not Alexander—only just a dinosaur!" Later, when I picked him up from school, his teacher seemed concerned. She wondered why he refused to talk in class. Alexander replied, "That's because dinosaurs don't talk!"

On a daily basis, I come to the conclusion that Jennifer is actually a thirty-four-year-old woman in the body of a four year old. What a wild woman! She performed in her very first ballet recital last month as a little snowflake in "The Littlest Nutcracker," and she had the time of her life. Each day she applies her make-up, has tea parties, and enjoys taking care of her "granddaughter," a doll she affectionately named Bucket Head.

Three-year-old Nicole loves to dance to Carly Simon's "You're So Vain," and when the verse "You walked into the party" comes, she screams "PARTY!" She then does the chicken dance. Nicole continues to love her stuffed pig, Winchester ("Witter"), who now has an equally adorable mate named Mabel, and she marches around with one pig nestled under each arm. She generally confines her artwork to walls and doors. One time, she decided that Alexander's favorite book was too heavy—"So I tooked out the extra pages."

I have been hopping between the washer, dryer, carpools, schools, and everywhere else within a thirty-mile radius of our town. In between my many obligations, I have done some freelance artwork, sung in coffee houses, and tried to keep up with my monogramming business. One monumental, yet exhilarating project I began this year was to illustrate and co-edit a cookbook to benefit the boys' school.

"Home" will be on another coast soon! This is bittersweet in so many ways. We will so miss all the close friends we have made here. Both girls were born here (in a hospital), as was our little lamb (in our pasture). Scott chose to name her "Gorgeous." When she broke her leg and ended up in our home as a bummer lamb for two months, all of us, including our nanny, joined in to help raise and feed her. None of us can forget when she literally ate Scott's homework! So many memories, so much fun, love, and laughter! Most importantly, we will keep these friends and memories in our hearts, as we move back east.

May the coming year bring only good health and contentment to you and those you dearly cherish. As for us, we find ourselves overwhelmingly grateful; for never could we dream of asking our Lord for all He has so generously blessed upon us. These blessings include you, our wonderful loved ones...

With love,
Will, Dana, Scott, Robert, Alexander, Jennifer and Nicole Andrews

CHAPTER 2

Flowers for My Mother

"This is what happens when you run."

These are the words I heard when seeking comfort from my mother after I tripped and fell, scraping my knees. Skinned knees were never kissed; they were another opportunity to be reminded that I should have known not to run. Apparently, I also should have known how to comfort myself...

Somewhere along the way, in the alchemy of my childlike thinking, I decided that since it wasn't working for me to expect my mother to make me happy, I would make HER happy. There was a little florist shop across the street from my junior high school. After school, I would run across the four-lane highway to the florist, where I could purchase two carnations for twenty-five cents. Then I'd run back across the four-lane street to catch the bus home, and I'd present them to my mother. One day, flush with money from a babysitting job, I got the idea to surprise her with roses instead of carnations. Unfortunately, buying the roses took a little longer than usual. As I sprinted back across the street with the roses, I saw the school bus pulling away.

I knew I was in trouble now. Instead of doing something to please her, I had done something that would bring down her wrath. I called my mother in tears, explaining that I missed the bus because I was buying her flowers. Coldly, she uttered two words: "Walk home." I walked the four long miles with a heavy backpack, a crushed heart, and two perfect pink roses. She refused them because she was angry with me. I told myself there was nothing she could ever do to take away the joy I got in buying them. At the same time, I felt like one of the thorns from the roses had pierced my heart.

In our poisonous house, gifts were a minefield, no matter who was giving them. I remember one experience as vividly as if it happened an hour ago. Mother had come home from shopping with Bianca. Mother took a beautiful bow-adorned box out of a fancy red bag and handed it to my sister.

"Well... open it, Bianca!" Bianca glared at me before removing the bow and showing me what was inside: a pink crystal atomizer with gold tassels suspended from a gold silken rope. I asked if I could have one too. "Maybe someday," my mother answered. "You don't need it now." I asked myself what "need" had to do with "want," and I wondered if any of my "needs" mattered. By then I knew the value of "someday" in the book of my mother's empty promises. Needless to say, I never received a pink crystal atomizer from my mother, or anything like it.

One day I asked my mother's permission to enter her bedroom. She was looking through her jewelry box. At the age of sixteen, I was becoming more interested in jewelry. As I looked at the beautiful pins, necklaces, and rings, she reminded me that all these beautiful things were from "Momma," my loving grandmother. "If you are good," she said, "one day these will be yours." Wasn't I good? What else could I try to do to prove that I was worthy of being in that category? Were my attempts unnoticed, or was I intrinsically undeserving of anything even remotely associated with the word "good?"

Among the sparkling gold pieces, I noticed a beautiful necklace, fashioned from an antique pocket-watch chain. Unbelievably, I summoned the courage to ask if I could have this chain. Her answer was painfully predictable: "You like this? Be good, and it will someday be yours."

I should have guessed what would happen next. At the dinner table that night sat Bianca, wearing that necklace. My heart dropped through the floor. Later that night I somehow managed to ask my mother why she had allowed Bianca to wear it. "I gave it to Bianca. She was born first." Yet more proof that my being born second made me second-class, not to mention a mistake.

I never did receive any of my grandmother's jewelry; it will all go to my sister and brother. The only thing my grandmother would ever pass on to me was something my mother couldn't take away. Although I hardly knew her, I always felt a kinship with my grandmother. She was a beautiful woman who lived in Canada, where my parents grew up and where Bianca and I were born. My memories of "Momma" end with her death when I was six years old. Her kindness and generosity provided reassurance; I would tell myself that I only imagined my mother was so mean—she was born to such a loving woman, surely she would show me her kind side. "Momma" was a loving and artistic soul, and I always felt that I inherited my appreciation for beauty and my artistic talent from her. Apparently, before she got married, she had hand-painted a silk robe and an entire set of china. My grandfather, who died when my mother was fourteen, was evidently a very bright, musically talented man, who played piano by ear, although I was told he was also very eccentric and obsessed with cleanliness. The musical and artistic talents I received from these grandparents would become my salvation, as I discovered the healing power of expressing my feelings through drawing and painting, writing, and playing music.

I also hope that I inherited my grandmother's kindness. Never could I intentionally or even unintentionally be mean to our children. Although the necklace and all the jewelry will belong to Bianca and Lawrence, Will buys me beautiful things that I know I will eventually pass on to our children. And it gives me so much pleasure to give gifts to our kids. I would never make them promises of something I don't intend to give them. Our children were born worthy of all good things, and I don't want them to feel they must toe the line in order to have something nice or something they want.

It may seem silly, but ice cream symbolizes this to me. My husband Will would tell me how, when he was a kid, he loved to eat coffee ice cream. Ice cream? In my house, we never had ice cream, let alone coffee flavor! When Will would mention how his mother always made sure there was plenty of chocolate syrup to accompany the ice cream, I was equally stunned. Chocolate syrup? Not in my house! For Will, these things were a given, an unremarkable pleasure of childhood. He didn't even have to skin his knee in order to qualify for this treat. This novel idea, that moms are supposed to WANT their kids to be happy, inspired me to create a family rule: we always have a huge supply of ice cream in many flavors, including coffee, as well as chocolate syrup. Ice cream is a given. Life has a way of rolling past way too quickly. Will and I will look for and find any reason there is to celebrate life and the little joys—like ice cream.

And in our house, gifts flow easily. Will and all of our kids send me flowers for Valentine's Day, birthdays, and Mother's Day. Nicole, our youngest, loves to bring me flowers from the garden, "just because." Children's generosity may be a natural thing, but it has to be loved into being, like any flower. Children are born wanting and needing to be loved. But their souls, like flowers, are fragile and easily crushed. No amount of water can resurrect a bruised bud; if you trample across a flowerbed, you cannot walk out of it backwards and un-trample the flowers. Our children will always know they are the cherished, magnificent flowers; they make our hearts rejoice.

The second family rule I made is that no one should ever cry alone. Rest assured, in the Andrews household we always have plenty of skinned knees, missed buses, and other reasons to be upset. As a child I cried myself to sleep too many nights to count. Our children know that no matter what, we will never run out of love, hugs, or ice cream. Will and I made sure that our children always knew they were cherished and never taken for granted. We feel that they are gifts from God. We do not own them; they are loaned to us so that we might raise them to become what they were created to be.

My kitchen has always been, for each of our children, the meeting ground for their friends. My kids knew that their friends were always welcome here; the more friends, the merrier. We had plenty of food. I would always be standing by the stove cooking, and they often took to calling Will and me "Dad" and "Mom." Our kids and their friends came to love the honest conversations, food tasting, and love that is generously given to all. They were welcome for anything, whether it was homework help, making a fun snack (caterpillar bagels with PB & J and carrot stick legs, for example), or listening to the highlights of their day. It gave my heart unequivocal joy to know that I was not only feeding their friends homemade meals, but I was feeding their hearts with an under-standing of belonging, an understanding that I had missed as a child. I was ful-filling my pact—with zeal! Coffee ice cream and chocolate syrup were the icing on the cake.

December 1996

Greetings!

Yes, it's that time of the year again, and this seemed to be the best way to:

    A – Let you know we are thinking of you,
    B – Apprise you of what we are up to,
    C – Give you something to read in the rest room,
    D – Give you some kind of clue as to why we are always LATE,
    E – Make your life seem completely sane,
    F – All of the above!

Last December we were preparing to move from our new (eight-year-old) home in Northern California to a big old (1740s) house in Massachusetts. We're finally here, and Main Street will never be the same!

After a relatively smooth cross-country move, we settled in rather quickly. I try so hard to remember what life was like back in California, but it already feels like we've lived here forever! We often speak of our good friends from places we've lived; they will always remain dear to our hearts. I tell our children that life is like a quilt—you gather good friends all along the way and each one becomes an integral piece of the most unique and beautiful heirloom called life.

I so cherish these cold and windy winter evenings when we eat dinner with a fire roaring in the hearth. I often wish these walls could speak, because I'd sure love to know what the original residents discussed at their dinner hour two hundred fifty years ago. Admittedly, it was challenging for the children to adjust to living in an older home. The wooden floors are authentic; I am always armed with tweezers and Band-Aids, ready to tackle the meanest of splinters. Some things were completely unexpected, like the presence of one or two spirits rumored to be earlier residents.

While the front of our home sits directly on Main Street (which is lined with many antique stores), the back of our property welcomes over thirteen acres of woods, which are home to deer and wild turkeys.

Scott is now eleven years old, and he attends seventh grade at a Friends School nearby. I am amazed by how well he helps to care for his siblings. No matter what he might appear to be doing, he is well aware of what his siblings are up to. I wonder if this might involve his wanting to protect his belongings from his siblings' sticky fingers… Often Scott's plans involve his younger siblings, for whom he assigns the more dangerous tasks, while he oversees the overall endeavor. The next thing you hear will be his assurance that he had nothing to do with the cries for help coming from a sibling stuck in a precarious position. Worry not; Scott already has a plan to save the day for a sibling in need!

Robert is now nine years old, and he enjoys fourth grade at the Friends School. I am quite amazed by the artistic talent Robert displays. His creations show accurate perspective and are so detailed and intricate. He has progressed from super-imposed photos of our faces on his cartoon drawings to drawing our faces with a great likeness, on the bodies of one another, complete with Nicole's beloved pigs. Those who know Robert well are familiar with his insatiable craving for candy. The main reason he was eager to move to Main Street was the apothecary two doors down from our home; to him it is the candy store.

Seven-year-old Alexander loves first grade at the Friends School. (I am convinced that they will name a whole wing at the school after us…) This happy little guy's curiosity about the solar systems, galaxies, and his environment is unending. He loves to read, and his favorite book is Treasure Island. Somehow, he has an ability to read anywhere, and he becomes so ensconced in his books that he is unaware of his surroundings. The biggest challenge we face with Alexander is that he is exceedingly quiet. When we are focused on his louder-than-life sisters, that is his cue to place his book on his lap, take an occasional bite of dinner, and read away.

Jennifer, now five, is both articulate and precocious; her preferred reading material would be Teen Beat *and* Martha Stewart Living! *At preschool, where Jennifer attends four days a week, she asked the Magic Pumpkin for three things: a car, a duck, and white hair. We know that when it comes to the girls, quiet = trouble. Will found both girls in their bedroom closet surrounded by little blond ringlets that looked much cuter on Nicole's head than on the closet floor. When she grows up, Jennifer longs to become a policewoman, but for the present, she has a double major: ballet and petty theft. She gracefully dances past her brothers while they are preoccupied with other endeavors, and then she snags enough of their possessions to fill her pockets.*

Nicole might be the baby, but she runs just as fast as her siblings. Both Jennifer and Nicole danced in their second ballet recital this past fall; Nicole decided (big surprise) to improvise her dance routine while onstage. There was little Nicole, spinning in circles and gathering snowflakes from the floor... Like her brother Alexander, she is very curious. Anything she gets her little hands on is taken apart, including Alexander's 500-piece Lego spaceship and my plants (have you never tasted a salad created from plant leaves?). Our pediatrician told me this is a sign of a bright and curious child, but her fearless free-spiritedness keeps us crossing our fingers that she will never end up incarcerated!

The one who keeps this place in line and maintains the moral decorum is Will. He is thoroughly enjoying his new position, and his work combines seeing patients, doing research, and teaching residents and medical students. Despite his rigorous schedule, Will's priority continues to be his family. It is a sight to behold when he walks in the door and all five kids push past me to get his first hug! After dinner, Will loves playing Magic Cards with Scott, practices piano with Robert and Alexander, and helps the girls locate all appropriated treasures they stashed in their room that need be returned to their brothers.

I seem to be running in many different directions, all at the same time! I am always late, but never one hour late! Recently I painted the walls: a mural of the beach in the children's bathroom, a wildflower path and cloud-filled ceiling in the girls' room, and a faux bookcase with tea cups in the hallway. I have especially enjoyed getting back into performing in coffeehouses. I am so grateful that in the midst of it all, I have written three songs in this past month! Surely the icing on the cake for which I am extremely grateful is a host of loving friends on Main Street, who've become surrogate sisters to me! We laugh and cry together...

It's so hard to believe that we've been married over fourteen wonderful and blessed years. Throughout the sunny days and stormy days, happy days and seemingly hopeless days, we trudge through, always remembering we are here for a reason—and that we are also here for one another!

May the miracle of the human spirit sustain and strengthen you through the struggles. We wish you a year filled with good health, lots of sleep, plentiful laughter, loving friends to share it with, and renewed dreams to carry you through it all...

All our love, Will, Dana, Scott, Robert, Alexander, Jennifer and Nicole Andrews

CHAPTER 3

My Room, My Sanctuary

"**G**et out of my sight. I don't even want to LOOK at you. Go to your room, you dumb bitch!"

Mother did her best to make me feel that my room was a place of punishment. I often heard words like this, and I knew better than to object to her orders. For my mother, my room was a place where she kept me out of sight. But not out of hearing: though my mother was heinously mean, unfortunately for me, she wasn't deaf. She would stand outside my bedroom door with two intentions—forcing me to hear the caustic messages she uttered through the door; but also listening to what I was doing. Whatever she could hear would then be reported to Bianca and anyone else who would listen. Always, my room-sentence would end with my father enlightening me on what I had "done wrong," and how stupid I was.

Yet, there was a silver lining to these confinements. Somehow, once I was in my room, I felt safe. This bedroom became not only a place to cry myself to sleep at night, a place to be confined when I had the audacity to assert my own thoughts and feelings. During the hours I spent alone in there, I developed the life-saving habit of drawing from the wellspring of my creative inner life. I drew pictures and painted. I took bits of fabric from my mother's ragbag and sewed them into dresses for my dolls. I vividly remember spending hours making paper shoes. This began when I was five, and Mother wouldn't allow me to get a new pair of shoes. I had to wear Bianca's old ones, and wait until she got new ones to replace them. I decided I would make my own, using paper and tape.

At first, my creative endeavors were an effort to gain my parents' attention and affection. But of course, this didn't work. The ragbag discards I cut and sewed into dresses for my dolls looked so beautiful to me, but garnered not even a nod when I proudly showed them to my mother—reminding me of my own status as a "discard," the unwanted child. Slowly, I learned to enjoy doing what I did for the pleasure it gave me alone.

The room gradually became my little secret garden. In my bedroom I had plants that thrived, and a multitude of paints, brushes, and canvases kindly given to me by an art teacher. This bedroom had two walls with windows to an outside world, where there must be others who were kind and could love me for who I was. It's no wonder that I imagined a wishing well in the middle of the room—a well of sustenance for me, where I could make wishes to live somewhere that I was valued and loved.

When I was outside, I also searched for a sense of sanctuary: some safe, hidden place underneath a tree or bush, like a little cove formed by branches. I would fill this little haven with beautiful things like daffodils and crocuses, and I would gather stones and mark a path to my happy home. This sweet womb of nature would be just roomy enough to hold me and my dreams. I fantasized that someday I would have a little cottage with walls of lavender, one of my favorite colors.

Although I was not allowed to change the colors of my room (I hated the red rug and black furniture), I constantly added things to surround myself with beauty. I brought in wooden fruit crates and stacked them up by the windows to hold all my favorite plants. The love for plants was the only thing I had in common with my parents. Unfortunately, that, too, was used against me. One Saturday morning my father came into my room, and he made a comment I will never forget: "Boy, with all these plants, one would think you are in competition with your mother." His words were so wrong, they made me feel sick. How could a psychiatrist who specialized in treating children and adolescents say such a hurtful thing? It stung even more to have them said in my room, the one place I felt safe. So much of what my parents said reminded me, "We cannot love you unless you change." To what? To whom? I desperately needed to be allowed to be me, and they couldn't or wouldn't do that.

As time went on, I learned to retreat to my room whenever the abuse would begin. But first, I needed to grab a glass of water. Once I closed the door of my room, I positioned my paints and brushes, dipped my brush in the water, let the paint flow. I would lose myself in that healing flow, watching my pictures emerge. Often, I would hear my mother from the other side of my door, unable to give up her ranting against me. I must have gotten used to hearing her mocking and belittling words. Somehow I used them, transforming their heat into an energy that breathed life into my paintings. Using brushes with as few as four or five bristles, I created images with the finest of detail. Hours later I would emerge from my room, recharged. Ever hopeful, I would show my parents my latest work of art, only to be greeted with disgust or indifference and the reminder that I was never to be forgiven or loved, "unless you change." Back to the brushes, paint, and canvases I went. The paintings I made were piled, one by one, under my bed—a slow layering of emotional scars, each one a failed attempt at showing my parents that, if nothing else, I was a good artist. At the same time, each one offering another chance to realize that in my hands I owned the ability to not only create beauty, but to someday climb out from the insanity of that household.

Yet, my mother sent me mixed messages about my artistic output, and this, too, may have helped me hold onto a shred of self-worth. Whenever she and my father had dinner parties, she would send me to bring my artwork to show their friends. Once I learned to sing and play guitar, she would often tell me to perform one of the songs I had written. When her friends would say that I was talented, her response was always the same: "At least she has *some* redeeming feature." Then came the dismissal to go back to my room. How was I good enough to perform for her friends and share my artwork with them, yet unworthy of all else?

The discovery that I could express my deep feelings through music led to my spending many hours singing, playing my guitar, and writing songs. And I did start to get appreciation for my artwork, as I began contributing still life drawings or pen and ink illustrations for our high school art magazine. As a teenager, it became harder and harder for me to live inside the punishing constraints of my life. One day, when I was sixteen, I decided I needed to get my own telephone—not just an extension, but my own telephone account that my mother wouldn't be able to eavesdrop on. I walked four miles to the closest phone company office, and I got a beautiful pink princess phone along with telephone service, which I paid for with babysitting money. What a glorious moment it was when I could finally have contact with the outside world from my place of incarceration!

One day, I found myself once again sentenced to my room. I don't remember what caused it this particular time—just that yet again, I had been unwilling to agree with Mother's opinion on something or appease her. In addition to belittling me, she was also constantly trying to rope me in to support her damning of others who had offended her by not agreeing to subject themselves to her behavior. I was just becoming increasingly unable to go along with her craziness. Using my new phone, I called Will. I had known him for about a year by then, and he had become not only my boyfriend, but my closest confidant. It felt so good to be able to unload the details of mother's latest drama to him—until I heard what sounded like a shoe kicking at my door. Mother began screaming at the top of her lungs, so loud that Will could hear on the other end of the line, how I was a "stupid bitch" who deserved nothing. She reminded me through my door that she really didn't care if I lived or died. That day she added, "If you died, the world would be a better place."

That day showed me that Mother had absolutely no boundaries, no limit as to how far she would go to try to break me. There was no safe place when it came to her. I was her punching bag, her "go to" whenever she felt endangered, or as she would always insist, "punished." Clearly, my taking this small step toward autonomy, breaking her cycle of control, freaked her out. Mother accused anyone who didn't concede to her of "needing psychiatric help." I could not win at a game where the rules changed at her every whim. I no longer wanted to win. I would just exist until I could be far, far away from her. I decided it was between God and me. Either He would save me from her, or He would help her out of her misery. I would not let myself be broken. She could continue to use her weapons, from yelling and belittling to withholding her love, but I would seek love from those who could someday love me unconditionally. I certainly would never find it within the walls of that house.

That was the day I wrote a song, "Get Out of My Life," that embodied my deep hurt and soothed my weary, beaten soul. The song was another attempt to understand what made my mother act the way she did. Mother was like a broken piece of china, with the pieces joined back together slightly out of whack, resting upon one another for support. One little eye roll, a slight nod of disapproval, and the pieces fell away from one another. It really didn't matter who the offender was. Maybe whatever glue had been used just wasn't up to the job of keeping her intact. Much as I wanted to, I was never able to find the glue that would hold her together.

The next day, as I walked down the hallway, I noticed something in my parents' bedroom. My mother had taped a note to the lampshade next to her bedside. It read, "I will not allow Dana into my heart or my mind. She does not exist." I wish I could forget those words. I knew from that day forward that there was no going back. I could be a part of her madness and survive. Somehow I had to learn to disengage from her punishing, poisonous behavior.

Those years of hiding away in my bedroom served me well; I never lost the sheer joy of making things and of making my surroundings more beautiful. I even gave myself permission to make bare walls my canvas.

This came in handy when our oldest boys were little, and Will and I purchased our first home. I wanted to spruce up the bare walls by putting up wallpaper. Will disagreed; ever practical, he felt that wallpaper wasn't a necessity—decorating the walls does not enhance their structural integrity! So, being who I am—tenacious and living by the motto, "if I cannot have it, I will *make* it"—I decided to create my own wall decoration.

Using wall paint and brushes, I began bringing the walls to life. In Scott and Robert's room I painted a life-sized old tree, adorned with vines climbing around the trunk. Placing my paint in paper cups lined up on the windowsill where they couldn't reach, I would paint while the boys would read their books and play. When the painting was done, I pushed thumbtacks along the vines so I could hang the boys' stuffed monkey collection in the tree. Robert and Scott saw nothing unusual in this. One day at their playgroup I overheard them talking with their friends.

"My mommy said we should NEVER color on my wall," one of the little boys said.

"Oh! My mommy doesn't think you should color either," Scott answered, then added, "She uses paints all over my walls. Tell your mom paint is better!"

Soon, other moms who brought their kids over for play dates would see the murals in our home, and word of mouth traveled. I began getting calls to paint in nurseries, stores, and doctors' offices. Soon I had a thriving mural business.

For me, painting is the most basic sustenance for my soul. When I paint, all is well with the universe. I become oblivious to all distractions, and time stands still. This was the gift I inherited from my maternal grandmother. My maternal uncle was a successful artist in Canada, known for his sculptures and prints. Neither my parents, nor my siblings, were blessed with artistic abilities, yet I can recall coloring, drawing, and painting with detail since the age of nine or ten.

Each time I paint is a celebration of my emergence from the dark cave I somehow escaped from, unbelievably, intact. Even now I love using oil paints to create a still life or some other subject, although I find it especially difficult to part with my paintings by selling them. But with murals, you have no choice! When you're done, you have to leave the walls with their rightful owners. I love working along with my clients to create exactly what they envision having in their home or office. I have painted everything from a lioness fountain (complete with a magnificent mane) in a hair salon, to a farm scene in a child's playroom. I've painted clouds on ceilings and "rugs" on wooden floors. Probably my favorite project was in our area upper elementary school. This was a "pro bono" job; I wanted to give back to this wonderful school where my kids had been nurtured. For this mural, I spent several months in the media center, illustrating quotes selected by the librarian. Some of these scenes were magical—a treasure trove of books and a castle entrance, with steps made from books. I painted a big tree on one wall, and then I asked the librarian if I could paint the four pillars in the room, using a four seasons theme. I did my very best on them, painting vines for each season: a bare vine adorned with cardinals, mittens, and a scarf for winter; autumn leaves and berries for fall; leaves, birds, and nests for the spring; and blooming wisteria flowers for summer. When I learned that the librarian was retiring that year and celebrating her fortieth wedding anniversary, I painted her husband's and her initials inside a heart at the base of the tree. When she saw this, she was brought to tears.

Somehow my heart is involved in every single mural I paint. I start by trying to capture what I see in the spirit of the commissioner, by playing twenty questions, teasing out what they envision but cannot describe. Once I have a general sense for what they want, ideas begin to fly into my head. Sometimes I will wake up in the middle of the night with ideas. It takes everything I have to stay in bed and not drive to the client's home, pull out my brushes, and start painting.

Over the years, I've been able to use this artistic blessing in many ways. I always designed our children's birth announcements, party invitations, illustrated the margins for some of my holiday letters, and made banners for a friend, who ran a marathon in honor of her daughter to raise money for pediatric cancer. When our oldest son Scott was in college, one of his friends passed away. I painted this young man's portrait on a long banner for his friends to sign and then give to his parents. One thing I learned from my own childhood nightmare: how, in the middle of heartbreak, I could draw from the well of creativity to find some solace, for me and for others.

December 1997

Greetings to you and yours!

Our motto has always been, "Things are always hopping at the Andrews household!" Well, this year they don't exactly hop—they walk, pace, trot, and answer to the names of Amber, Kyra, Bandit, and Nino. Yes, we have four beautiful llamas! The main feature on our menu these days is alfalfa hay and carrots. Once spring rolls around, there will be a direct line between their fleece and my spinning wheel.

This past year was filled to overflowing with school activities, sports, music lessons, and religious studies. Somehow, it remains difficult to be consistent with anything except for being late for everything always! This is probably the fifth year that a helicopter will be first on my holiday wish list. A pilot would be nice, too...

In addition to renewing old friendships, we made many new ones. Friends are the foundation of life; they make rainy days fun, and weekends disappear into thin air. This was the year I learned to put down the broom, open the door, and let in the laughter (via my hysterically funny neighbor who makes life worth living). The best thing about friends is that they help you through the sad times, too. This year was a bittersweet one; we all watched helplessly as close family friends lost their ten-year-old daughter to cancer. This beautiful girl touched so many people, and her memory continues to warm our bruised hearts. I believe Heaven has given her the most exquisite wings.

It's hard to believe we moved here two years ago! We love this old home, and we still ponder what the 18th century residents did in their spare time. With regards to the séance I had hoped for, let me tell you a little story... One night, while I stayed at the kitchen table cutting the children's food on their plates, I mentioned to Will, who was at the kitchen bar area pouring the glasses of milk, that I wished to have a séance so we could learn more about the supposed spirits (a.k.a., ghosts!) rumored to be living in our home. Will simply stated, "Not going to happen. First off, it will scare the children. Secondly, I do not believe in ghosts!" At this point, all the glasses began to fall out of the open cabinet. Will looked white (as a ghost) and freely admits that he has now changed his mind about ghosts.

We continue to treasure family dinners by the hearth. Even the cats have their own special spot in my yarn-filled grain bin. When I see Will and all five children gathered around the dinner table, I have to pinch myself underneath the table.

Scott is now twelve, and he is currently in eighth grade. He plays electric guitar, soccer, basketball, and is eagerly preparing for his Bar Mitzvah next May. His sharp wit and equally sharp mind serve to keep him in good form. It amazes me when I see how adept he is with the computer we won in a newspaper contest. Jennifer and Nicole crayoned all over the instruction manual; Scott still had the computer unpacked and in running order within an hour! He is extremely helpful with his chores. One day recently, he fed the llamas before going to school. For some reason, one of the llamas woke up on the wrong side of the pasture, and it decided to spit all over poor Scott! It was pretty funny writing a note to the headmaster explaining why Scott was so late for school.

Robert is now ten years old, and he enjoys fifth grade. There are always either drumsticks or a pencil in his hands or pocket: he plays drums and continues to express his artistic gifts, constantly drawing cartoons and detailed real-life renderings. Robert is always the first to offer a hug to those in need of emotional rescue. A friend of Robert's came to school in tears recently because his mother told him they could not keep all their cat's kittens. "Don't worry," Robert reassured him. "Tell your mom we would love to keep them all! We will even keep them fed and warm!" Fortunately all but two were earmarked. We named these two black kittens Sara and Sydney. Robert takes such responsibility for them, apologizing for their misdeeds as they are running amok. Even if his kittens make me nuts, Robert makes my heart smile.

Alexander is now seven, and he's in second grade at school with his brothers. Alexander will read anything, and he excels at both piano and his studies. With an amazing compassion for all living things, this sweet child is on a mission to save all spiders and bugs from the fate of the great Hoover. Recently he observed me vacuuming the floor, and he noticed several ants. Immediately he ran to unplug the vacuum, and he declared crossly, "Ants are living creatures, too, Mom! You must not destroy them!" While I stood speechless, he grabbed a dustpan and brush to aid in their rescue.

Jennifer is almost six years old, and she attends kindergarten, while minoring in petty theft. On a daily basis, she appropriates her siblings' allowance and toys, but she's most adept at sharing her hugs and kisses with all. She loves to have play dates with her friends, but her passion is wrestling on the floor with Alexander. She is no shrinking violet! When she fears she might not have the upper hand, she stops and warns, "Don't mess with me!" She decided that Bucket Head is for babies and tossed her to the very back of her closet, along with the scissors she used to cut Nicole's hair last year (and Nicole's favorite Barbie's hair last week). When she grows up she wants to be a "police lady" and also a "lady who cleans dogs."

Nicole is now four, but she thinks she's a grown woman. She has decided that she wants to be a movie star when she grows up (as in tomorrow). She struts through life wearing plastic high heels and mismatched short sets. This morning she reported to me, "The coffeepot is snoring. How will the coffee wake you up now?" While we were vacationing, Nicole, seemingly bored with our company, decided to take a very long (over one mile) stroll. Picture this blonde, curly-haired toddler in her hot pink polka dotted bikini strutting along the beach... We feared we might never see her again and were panic-stricken. Fortunately we summoned the police, who found her taking her solitary Sunday stroll. She seemed to enjoy her ride home via police car.

This brings us to Will. This guy is the glue that holds us together. Will is always there to ensure everyone is happy, including the animals. India and Iman believe they own Will's heart, since he is the one who supplies endless treats and the occasional loafer that ends being their rawhide. He does the majority of driving the kids forty-five minutes away to their Hebrew School. He imparts such a sense of humility and integrity to our children. We are so blessed by this wonderful husband and father.

I've been busy… It seems I find myself singing "Climb Every Mountain" each day, as I climb mountains of laundry in a frantic attempt to fold and sort it all! When I find time, I still find much joy in sewing matching dresses for the girls, but it seems I am most fulfilled when I have a paintbrush in my hand and a bare wall in front of me (ceilings will do as well). Recently I resumed songwriting; my most recent song is "Breath of Morning." My next song will be called "Lost in the Laundry of Life!" I also served on the Parent-Teacher Organization, and I was asked to coordinate the Back To School Picnic. I daydream about getting some sleep. You'll never find me complaining; there will never be enough time, paper, or pencils to list my gratefulness for it all, and for you, our cherished loved ones!

We all send you our heartfelt love and our warmest wishes for a year filled with good health, laughter, and plentiful hours spent with those you hold dear. A ton of uninterrupted sleep wouldn't be so bad either!

Until we can bore you next year,
All our love,
Will, Dana, Scott, Robert, Alexander, Jennifer, and Nicole Andrews

CHAPTER 4

The Family Table

"Dana, you constantly monopolize the conversation," my mother said. "No one really cares about these stupid stories."

We were sitting around the dinner table, as we did on most nights—my mother at one end, my father at the other, and the three kids on either side. Lawrence was three by then, and I was nine. Our dinner conversations followed a pattern: my mother would ask my father which patients he saw that day and what their current issues were. She would then go on about how terrible their parents must have been, for their children to have such problems. Then they would ask Bianca about her day. She shared only what she wanted them to know. She never told them about the parties she went to or how she never did her schoolwork. No matter what she did or did not do, she was unequivocally their favorite.

But when I spoke up to talk about my day, my mother would cut me off. As a child, I looked forward to telling stories about my day with my family at the dinner table. Maybe because I enjoyed the time I was away at school, I would come home feeling happy, and I wanted to share that with my parents and siblings. Maybe I just couldn't let go of my inner sense of fairness—if everyone else could talk, why not me? When Mother cut me off like this, I would immediately clam up, my hurting heart giving way to silent tears. The next night, being tenacious, I would try again, hoping maybe this time my mother would allow the rest of my family to listen, and they would realize that my stories *were* worthy of being heard. This scenario repeated itself again and again, and my feelings took their free-fall night after night.

A few nights later, I spoke up again. To my surprise, this time the nightly dinnertime reprimand didn't come. I talked on happily, describing everything I could remember about my day: which friend I ate lunch with, and how I did in my school subjects. Everyone seemed to be listening intently to what I had to say. Finally, my family realized that I did have important thoughts to bring to the table—I was worthy of their attention!

My mother's expression suddenly changed, and she exchanged a nod with my father and my sister. Then she bent over and reached for something underneath the dinner table. I hadn't noticed anything drop. From under the table, she retrieved a tape recorder, along with a microphone dangling from it by a black cord. As she placed it down, my body went cold and numb, and I realized it was suddenly very quiet at the table—I had lost the ability to speak, or even to think straight. Had I said something terribly wrong, broken some rule I didn't know of? I only knew I was in big trouble now. My instincts were screaming for me to run, to get away from what was about to happen, but I saw my mother and Bianca had gotten up to block my means of escape—they each stood by a doorway, as my father ordered us all to sit down.

"Do not dare move from your seat," Mother warned me. "You *will* listen to this. You need to hear how much you monopolize the conversation every night."

She pressed rewind, and soon after, the play button. As my recorded voice issued from the tape recorder, mother offered a running commentary: "See? There you go again! What ever gave you the idea that anyone would ever care to hear *anything* you wanted to say?" Then my voice was heard again. "Look at you! I don't even want to look at you, let alone hear your voice." Through all this, Bianca watched with eager glee.

I understood what a sick prank they had pulled off—this had all been planned ahead of time. But part of me couldn't believe they would go this far at my expense. They abhorred me, yet loved making me into their fool. How could you ridicule your child like this? They easily could have taken me aside and explained that I should give time to others to share their day at the dinner table. Instead they had blindsided me, tearing me apart in this very public way, all the while acting as if they had the moral high ground. I was mortified, devastated, and shaking with anger.

I crumpled my dinner napkin into a tiny ball. How could my father offer his professional services as a child and adolescent psychiatrist during the day, yet leave it all at his office and return home as a willing participant in my mother's abuse? Where was his heart, his conscience? How could he allow my mother to shred my confidence this way?

I stood up to leave. As I walked past my father, he chuckled at me. I took the balled-up napkin and threw it at his face. Maybe I hoped this would wake him up and make him see what he was doing to his own child. His reaction was pathetic: he joined in with Mother and Bianca in plentiful laughter. They all but gave me a standing ovation for the entertainment I provided for them. I went to my room, feeling both angry and empty.

This experience had given me a profound lesson. In my family, things would never be normal or fair; if anything, they would become even worse. My mother was heartless, cruel, and coldblooded. I would never be safe with her. She would continue to use me as her voodoo doll, sticking pins in me to appease her own demons. She would always find another way to strike, paralyzing me with shame and pain. It was a terrible lesson for a sensitive nine year old to learn.

At the same time, precisely because I had no way to predict which behaviors of mine would be met with resistance or punishment, somehow I concluded that I might as well go ahead and do what I felt was necessary and right. Looking back, I'm thankful that my inner compass pointed me toward choices that eventually led me to love and happiness. Even then, I could not find it within me to take on their behavior as my own. I could never do to others, even them, what they did to me. Doing this would surely never possibly undo the evils they perpetuated daily.

I began to feel as if the two parents and two siblings I lived with were "family" in name only. To them I was an encumbrance, someone who should be neither seen nor heard. Over and over I had received the message that I was not wanted, not appreciated, and didn't matter. The only joy these people seemed to get from my presence was found in mocking and belittling me.

It was not long after this experience at the dining room table that I lay in bed one night and made my pact with God. Obviously He was the only one who *did* want me to be here; the only one who would hopefully listen without mocking me. He was the only one who could help me now.

But things would get worse before they got better. Starting around this time, I feared my mother and sister so much that I routinely wet my pants before returning home from school each day. This continued until I turned twelve. I would run as fast as I could to my room to get changed so they would not know. Each time I entered the house, it felt like I was voluntarily walking into a lion's den. In some twisted way, Mother and Bianca made me feel that I lived there only by their permission, that I deserved and was even asking for their abuse. Yet I never did get used to their all-too-consistent torment.

As time went on, my mother and sister's games became even more sadistic and shameless. Although I knew to expect their ridicule and plots against me, I never knew when, how, or even how far they would go. Their audience grew to include anyone we knew. They would take turns contacting relatives and friends to inform them of my latest "trick." Anything I did or said, from their point of view, was intended to inconvenience or annoy them. It was always me who was at fault. When Bianca and I were teenagers, I walked into my room one day and found Bianca using the makeup I bought with my hard-earned babysitting money. I asked her why she was in my room and why she never asked to use my things. Immediately she got up and went to Mother, and she began complaining that I was being mean to her. Mother stomped up the stairs and down the hall to my room. She then informed me that I didn't deserve to have this makeup, but Bianca did. Once again I was sentenced to my room for not sharing and for being mean to my sister. As always, the routine was not complete until Bianca gloated in my face, sometimes with my mother and father joining in. I always tried to leave, knowing I was being set up once again, but that was against their rules. They seemed to be addicted to seeing me humiliated and tormented, to playing a game in which I always lost. Losing meant going to my bedroom, where I had to cry silently, since they would be standing by my door—if they could hear me, there would be more mockery.

For me, the toll was tremendous. One unfortunate effect I began to develop was a kind of delayed reaction to these intense experiences; sadly this continues with me to this day. As soon as I knew a confrontation was looming, my body would turn cold and my mind would go blank. Even though I knew what was about to happen was wrong, I would temporarily shut down emotionally; it could be hours or even days afterward before I was able to piece together the scenario of what had played out and begin to process the emotions it triggered. This may have begun as a defense mechanism; at the time, I think I wanted to hold in any reaction, to deprive them of the pleasure of seeing me suffer. For all the pain and anger they caused me, I did not want to play their games. Somehow, my emotional withdrawal may have protected that little, secret part of me that I felt I still owned: my inner dreams of one day being happy. Someday, I told myself, I would escape them and claim my life for myself. There was no way out until I could be on my own, away from them.

The other effect was even worse than that: having nowhere to place my anger, I turned it inward on myself. If they were right, and if I hated myself more than they hated me, then it would be easier to tolerate their vicious behavior towards me. In a sick way, it gave me the psychological upper hand. My inner voice became a duet; one side sang the tune that had kept me alive, "You are surrounded by a bunch of people who will not ever get you, no matter what you do," while the other side sang the dissonant harmony, "Here we go again... You are living a lie. You will never be worthy, no matter how hard you try." Those two voices played opposite each other in my head way too often. Sadly, I still hear the negative side now sometimes, years after leaving home and making my own life.

But as long as their abuse continued, my self-directed anger grew stronger. Anything that happened gave me another reason to blame myself and hate myself. When I would forget to bring my homework to school, I became furious at myself, and I would tell myself that I was better off dead. When I was in seventh grade, I got my period for the first time at school. The nurse, trying to help me deal with a deeply embarrassing situation, called my mother and asked her to bring me clean pants. My mother refused, telling me I was pathetic and she had better things to do. My reaction? I berated myself for being so stupid. This, too, was *my* fault. I went to the rest room and cleaned my pants, deciding it was my fate to wear wet pants in school.

Experiences like this left me seeing myself as a completely flawed being, deserving only of rejection and mockery. I never expected approval or love, and when I did get it I was sure it was fake—part of a cruel game that would end in another painful lesson. If I kept my expectations at that ridiculously low level, the always-impending fall would not be as devastating.

This terrible experience will never fully leave me. And it has had a deep impact on my mothering—as a counterexample. I will never silence our children's voices; I cherish not only who they are, but also what they have to say. As they each grow into themselves, I encourage them to know that their own opinions, life experiences, and whatever they wish to share are valued. More than anything else, we deeply respect their personhood. We try always to build them up, not tear them down. And we have tried to instill in them the lesson I somehow took from my childhood: above all, be kind and generous, make sure others know they matter, and show appreciation every day for anything you can possibly find to be thankful for.

December 1998

This holiday letter probably finds you whirling in the holiday hustle. Hopefully it will also find you an opportunity to find a furry blanket and some hot cocoa, so you can sit for a spell! Leave the rest to me as I update you on all that is new in the last 364 days. Oh, what a ride!

This past year marked so many firsts for all of us. Five-year-old Nicole entered kindergarten and learned how to tie her shoes, add, subtract, and spell. She is most proud of her recent accomplishment: she taught herself how to whistle! When not intently whistling, Nicole loves to sing... at the top of her lungs. Although she will tell you, "I am a growed-up lady now," when she grows older she aspires to be a singer, a teacher, and "a princess with a beautiful dress, and long, straight hair with a sparkly bow." (With her curly blond tresses, we call her "curly Shirley.") This loyal little lady continues to cuddle her beloved pigs, Winchester and Mabel-Rose.

This fall was a big first for six-year-old Jennifer, as she entered first grade at Friends School. She enjoys caring for all of our pets. Jennifer tells us that when she grows up, she wants to "be a police lady and also maybe a scientist who studies dinosaurs." Nightly, Jennifer, Nicole, and I snuggle on their window seat and tell our favorite fairy stories. On one occasion Jennifer overheard her brothers talking about how fairies are not real. She informed them that they are to never say that again. Doing this "would break my heart. And besides, who else would be eating the little apple pieces I leave for them, and leave behind such sparkly fairy dust?" The most magical part of the day is at night, when a silence falls over our household. When my two little sweethearts fall fast asleep, I love to sneak back into their room just to watch them softly sleeping.

Wishing to never sleep and to stay awake all night reading, is nine-year-old Alexander, excelling in third grade at the Friends School. When asked to use caution on the monkey bars at school, Alexander replied, "Oh... But Danger is my middle name!" He loves to rhyme, using this skill in daily conversation. When he calls for me, it is not simply "Mom." It would more likely be, "Hey! Mom, you are a bomb who went to the prom with Dad.com in Viet Nam..." In case of hunger or thirst, he is a man of few words; he will put down his book and run to me, saying "Parched" or "Seeking sustenance!" When he grows up, Alexander aspires to be an inventor and work for the CIA. Until then, we'll just keep those heaping bowls of ice cream and adventure books in sufficient supply.

Eleven-year-old Robert continues to attend Friends School, and he's now in sixth grade and having the time of his life. Robert has shown an avid interest in drama—he received rave reviews in "The White Glove" this past summer. He has become quite a drummer; occasionally he and Scott and another friend get together to have "band practice." Robert is extremely social, yet often reveals his sensitive side. Whenever a classmate or teacher from school is sick, he will make them an elaborate and humorous get well card. Recently he made a card for a friend with chicken pox. On this large poster board he drew hundreds of red polka dots ("They are supposed to look like chicken pox!"), and he advised his friend to "connect the dots" if he got bored.

It is hard to believe Scott is now thirteen years old! This past May, Scott became a Bar Mitzvah; his performance was excellent and incredibly touching. We were so proud that day—it was wonderful to have all the children involved in the service. The reception that followed the service was in our barn; we hung beautiful quilts on the barn walls, making it a warm and unique place to dance the night away. There is such a quiet sweetness in Scott, especially when he prepares cheese omelets for his siblings and assists them with homework, or when he takes them outside each evening to feed the llamas. He gently lifts up Nicole so she can feed them hay; she tells me this is why Scott is her hero!

Most of the time, Will and I wander about at home feeling akin to zombies, due to major sleep deprivation! Will somehow functions exceptionally well when at work (thankfully, especially for his patients). He is on staff at three area hospitals, and he offers his staff and patients the same kindness and compassion as he gives his family at home. He is there to celebrate the little joys that thrill us, laugh at the practical jokes courtesy of our in-house jokers, and keep us in line when we all run amok.

This past summer we celebrated our sixteenth wedding anniversary! We spent several weeks on a family vacation to the beach, boating, swimming in the lagoon, bowling, seeing movies, and dining out at wonderful seafood restaurants. Our yearly beach excursions make it easy to forget all the responsibilities inherent in the school year schedule. Mostly, we prefer our nightly dinners by the fire; they are always overflowing with spilled milk, funny stories, commentaries, and Will and me begging the kids to eat vegetables.

Each day I seem to be busier than the day before. Forget about sleep; laundry seems to be my middle name. This year I was asked to design a wedding canopy and Torah mantle to commemorate the thirty-fifth anniversary of our synagogue, and I'm helping with the quilting and needlepoint of these projects. I was also asked by the school to help the children create a first grade quilt to be sold at the annual auction. I am team leader for Wild Women of Wonder, and I get so much pleasure in working with such articulate and capable women! Recently my team members and I offered our services at an area hospital, where we taught skin care, make-up application, and gave hand treatments to women undergoing chemotherapy. It was a most humbling experience... This past August I performed my newest songs while accompanying myself on guitar, at a bookstore café nearby. I live each day reminded of our plentiful blessings. I am especially grateful for the wonderful and fulfilling relationships I have made this past year.

And we remain ever thankful that in this spinning maze, our spirits and yours have found and touched one another. May you always feel the warmth of our souls, sense the love in our hearts, and hear the melody of the song that keeps us dancing through life. We dearly cherish you!

With all the love from our happy little souls,
Will, Dana, Scott, Robert, Alexander, Jennifer and Nicole Andrews

CHAPTER 5

Goodbye, Tammy

When I was a child, I often dreamed of having a pet to love and be loved by. But my parents—particularly my mother—did not embrace the idea of having animals. My mother said that they were dirty, and we "didn't need one." At one point, when my sister and I begged to have a pet, they gave in: they got us a turtle. I can't even remember what we named this "pet," but I do remember observing that it did not really seem to have much of a life in its little glass bowl. I also remember thinking that his hard shell did not lend itself to be stroked, let alone cuddled. Later on, we got another turtle, and eventually we got a goldfish.

When I was eight, a happy accident sent us something more like what I wished for. Friends of my parents didn't have enough time to care for their six-year-old miniature poodle, and they gave her to us. Finally we had a real pet! Tammy was the sweetest little dog, and I fell in love with her instantly. She was particularly fond of my father, whose softhearted soul she recognized. My mother, on the other hand, was another story. As a housekeeper Mother was overly clean and controlling—an understatement—and she took Tammy's behavior as a personal affront. Little Tammy would be reprimanded when she tracked mud or leaves into the house on her paws, as well as for similar infractions. The dog soon sensed that my mother was definitely not her fan. Unfortunately, when my mother would yell at or smack this sweet dog with a rolled-up newspaper, Tammy would run from room to room, a bundle of nerves, and urinate on the rug.

One day, returning from school, I noticed Tammy hiding underneath my mother's car. My instincts screamed that something was amiss, but my eight-year-old mind hoped I was wrong. I gently pulled her out from under the car and carried her inside. My mother stood at the doorway, holding her purse and car keys.

"Let's go," she said. "This dog must go. We are taking her to the SPCA and leaving her there. I can't stand her."

Off we went to the SPCA. I will never, ever forget that drive or what happened next. We took her into the building, where there was a deafening noise of many dogs barking and whimpering. I whimpered and cried even louder, so my voice carried over the dogs. I begged and pleaded with my mother. I offered to clean the rugs. At a certain point I realized that this was not about me at all. There was nothing I could possibly promise, offer, or beg for to save Tammy. I keenly felt the gulf between my mother's personal needs and what I wanted so strongly.

My mother would not allow me to say goodbye as she handed our frightened, shaking dog over to the girl behind the desk. She grabbed my hand to leave. As we walked past the fenced-in area, I saw Tammy among the other forlorn-looking dogs. Poor Tammy. She stood up against the fence and cried. I wished that this moment were not real. The only real pet I had ever known—this dog I had so quickly fallen in love with—was being abandoned, and I couldn't even say goodbye. The whole way home I had to listen as my mother enumerated all the reasons that we should never have taken this dog. "Dogs are only trouble. Because of her we will have to get the rugs cleaned." I knew better than to answer her, but I thought to myself that dirt and urine can be cleaned, but what could mend my bruised heart? I never saw Tammy again.

It wasn't until years later that I was able to get a pet that was mine to love. When Will and I were first married, he brought home two little calico kittens—sisters from the same litter that had been found in a window well. They were so cuddly, and we enjoyed their spunky and often wild antics. When our family had grown to include three little children, we moved to Northern California, settling into a rented townhouse. With three active little boys, we soon realized we needed to move into a house. We looked for a place with plenty of room for the children to run around, and we found a big ranch house on five acres. During a meeting with our mortgage agent, she mentioned she lived on a farm, and that she had some sheep. Will gave me a look that translated roughly as, *we're only here for our mortgage—do not get started about her sheep!* My next words, of course, were, "Did you say you have sheep?" By the end of the meeting, our mortgage was a done deal, and I had worked out another deal—this kind woman would sell us several ewes, as well as lend us her ram. Will was not thrilled; I, on the other hand, was ecstatic.

Within several days, Will came around. He went to the feed store near our new home and bought some books on raising sheep. We put in fencing, and the sheep arrived. Soon we were purchasing many bales of alfalfa hay. One day Will went out to feed the sheep and found that one of our ewes had given birth to triplets—three tiny white lambs sitting in the middle of the pasture! The kids were enthralled with this miracle. We soon decided to round out the farm by adding chickens, turkeys, and ducks to our little menagerie. When on a run to the feed store, Will noticed a litter of black border collies needing a home. He brought two puppies home. The kids instantly fell in love with them. It seemed as if the more animals were part of our household, the more love there was to go around.

One day, when I was eight months pregnant with our fifth child, Nicole, I noticed that one of our ewes looked pregnant too. When Will came home later, he thought she was getting close to delivering. Pointing out that I'd had more experience in childbirth, he suggested I help her out. (He was kind enough to hand me some heavy-duty rubber gloves.) I did my best to help her deliver her young, but being so pregnant, I could barely get close enough to help her. We finally called the vet, who came out to help us. Sadly, both of her babies were already stillborn, and she was very sick. We were able to nurse her back to health, and she had more babies—though not delivered by me.

Our experience with the sheep opened the barn door, along with the door to Will's kind heart. A few years later, we moved back east to Massachusetts, and into our wonderful old house on thirteen acres. The move promised many good things for us: the children would be able to get to know their grandparents and cousins, Will and I would be back near the area where we were raised, and our family would once again be able to experience four distinct seasons—along with snow, a first for the kids. Will's father is also a physician, and Will would be practicing at the hospital where he was trained and where his father still worked.

It turned out that a physician who practiced with Will's dad happened to own some llamas. When he found out we had a lot of pasture land, he generously offered us four llamas. Will embraced the idea. As with the sheep, we quickly put up fencing and ordered bales of hay. Our children really took to them. That first year in New England, we took a different kind of family picture to accompany our holiday letter: it showed all the kids lined up by age, each holding a carrot, with the llamas lined up behind them. Each of the kids learned how to care for the llamas; they also learned what to do when the llamas would shift their ears back—run like the wind and not turn back because the llama was getting ready to spit! It was fun having llamas—unless you had to feed them, groom them, or shear them, in which case you might end up getting spat on by said llamas. They did, however, enjoy our daily walks, when I would put them on leashes and walk up and down Main Street. They didn't mind cars and trucks, but dogs were, for them, yet *another* invitation to spit.

Once, the kids chose to bring the llamas for their show and tell. I walked our llamas up the street to their school, lugging a huge sack full of hay and a bag of carrots. Fortunately, the llamas were in a pleasant mood that day, and our children and their peers had a great time bonding with our fickle pets. Scott and Robert, our two oldest, loved using the llamas to their advantage. When their sisters were doing homework, both boys would walk the llamas back and forth past the sliding glass doors by the girls' desks, sending them into fits of giggles.

One day we found one of the llamas gravely ill in the back of the pasture. We had no clue as to what happened to make her this sick, and we immediately called the vet. When he came out, we answered his many questions, which sounded mostly benign. Yes, we fed her alfalfa hay, and sometimes we fed her carrots. Yes, she had access to plenty of water, and no, the kids did *not* give her chocolate or candy. (Robert protested that he would never have shared his beloved stash with them.) Then the vet picked up a large branch lying nearby and asked how it got there. Will told the vet he had trimmed the bushes and given the branches to our llamas, since there were no trees for them to munch on in our pasture. The vet looked sharply at Will and asked if the branch happened to be from a rhododendron bush. Will confirmed that it was. The vet then told us that these bushes are very poisonous to llamas. Who knew? We certainly hadn't.

With Will going off to work, I added nursing the llama to my household duties. I had to go out into the pasture every two hours to force-feed this ailing llama, using a syringe to feed her a dose of strong coffee. The kids did their bit to help: Scott covered her with his brother Robert's Star Wars blanket, Alexander offered to read to her, Jennifer tried to hand feed her little torn pieces of hay, and Nicole offered to allow her to snuggle with one of her stuffed piggies. This story had a sweet ending: our persnickety llama thrived.

It took many years before it dawned on me: animals are as vulnerable as I was throughout my childhood. Having animals meant yet another chance to undo the traumatic circumstances I endured for years, by lavishing unconditional love on creatures as helpless as I had been then. It also provided me the opportunity to welcome the unfolding of nature, completely unaffected by external control and manipulation. I had never thought of myself as an animal lover, but throughout the years I have found tremendous enjoyment, not to mention emotional comfort, from our various pets. As I write this, our sweet little miniature pig sleeps peacefully on my lap, while our dogs nap on the couch nearby. How wonderful it is to know that they trust my love for them. They don't know cruelty, and I will make sure they never will. I delight in making them happy. The simple act of feeding them—carrots to our pig and our dogs, chicken scratch and other tasty treats to our chickens, and frozen peas (their favorite!) to the ducks—fills my heart with happiness.

December 1999

Greetings!

Our family motto is still, "Things are always hopping in the Andrews household." Well, this past summer our entire household took a major hop! Had someone told me last November we would be moving again, I'd have accused that person of looking into the wrong crystal ball. Needless to say, we survived the move, and we're so happy to be here. As for the llamas, they hopped elsewhere; they are now spitting on someone else...

Our previous residence was a house; our new humble abode is a home. It is a colonial farmhouse built in 1831, situated on two acres. It has such a cozy feel to it, and our new neighbors aren't antique stores—we live in a neighborhood of friendly people and lots of children. Despite the craziness of our move in early August, we've learned, laughed, and loved throughout all the seasons. Yes, there were many rainy days, but they always make the flowers grow.

Speaking of growing, Scott, who turned fourteen this past July, is now taller than Will and me! He has adapted to his new surroundings so well. Although a year younger than most of his peers, he enjoys tenth grade and has become increasingly social. Aside from remaining on the computer from dusk until dawn, his hobbies include playing electric guitar, basketball, and roller hockey. Although he has definitely entered the teen years (where chores are only for siblings but food is reserved for Scott) he continues to excel in all he undertakes, and he maintains a balanced perspective. His motto illustrates that well: "Trust me! I might get you into trouble, but I will always get you out!"

Scott and his brothers occupy the third floor, each in their own room. Even in total darkness, you can easily find Robert's room by following the sound of drumming. At twelve years old, our little drummer boy is thriving and loves seventh grade. He plays piano by ear, writes songs, loves performing in plays, and continues to illustrate with amazing perspective and detail. Robert has developed the ability to impersonate others to a T. He does a mean *Nicole impression: complete with the high-heels tiptoe, curtsey, and hair fluffing, in a high voice, Robert declares, "Nobody should mess with my pink purse, my piggies, or my Fairy Princess Tiara!"*

The third occupant of the third floor is nine-year-old Alexander. Enjoying fourth grade, this happy guy seizes every day. In the past year, he has developed an insatiable passion for reading 500-page novels, rhyming (his siblings had hoped this was just a passing fancy last year), and wreaking havoc on the computer and Nintendo. It is not uncommon to find Alexander walking around us in circles while gesturing and philosophizing on a given phenomenon. While he is explaining the mechanics of, say, a turbine imparting rotational energy to a rotor, Jennifer tells him to "cut to the chase! It's wrestling time!" Then you'll find them wrestling each other on the floor, often amid roars of laughter.

Jennifer has made a seamless adjustment to elementary school. She played soccer (an undefeated season!) and recently qualified for a position on the traveling soccer team. I often find myself mesmerized by how Jennifer, wanting to be a tomboy, hides so much emotion and sensitivity behind her long, dark hair and enormous brown eyes. I long to watch the years unfold to reveal the magic that emanates from Jennifer's heart; when we snuggle together, there is simply nothing amiss in our world...

And now... enter six-year-old Nicole, the one with the potential to turn the world upside-down! Nicole continues to profess her undying love for her stuffed pigs. Mabel and Winchester get tucked into Nicole's sleigh bed each morning, and they spend each night tightly squeezed within her grasp. Nicole's pendulum swings wide; much of the time she's whistling and enjoying life. At other times she becomes wistful; recently she informed me "we should always listen to our heart..." Nicole loves first grade, and she enjoyed playing soccer last fall. Really, she would much rather be playing with Barbie or coloring with crayons, or putting together her wild, crazy getups, imaginative hair-dos, and artistic make-up applications.

Between school, religious school, and sports commitments, the kids and I try to visit our two "adopted" seniors at the geriatric center nearby. Scott thinks these visits leave no impact, since the same ladies ask us who we are each time we visit! Robert studies these sweet little old ladies, making mental pictures of their toothless grins and kind gestures, to get their impersonations down pat. Alexander brings his book and fails to hear or respond when asked what he is reading. Jennifer yells at him, accusing him of pretending to be deaf like the ladies are. Nicole brings her Mary Poppins bag full of shoes and outfits, and she plays show and tell with all of our ladies. Alexander informed her that old people try to be nice to annoying little girls like her. Scott decided it was time to gain some perspective: "When you think about it, all that matters is that we are making old hearts happy!"

Will, the one we all adore, continues to enjoy his medical practice. He embraces the academic side of medicine, and he continues to write chapters for various books and articles for journals. It is one of the greatest joys of my day when Will comes walking in the door and five sets of feet make their way to greet Daddy! He comes home from a long day at the hospital, drops his briefcase, and lies on the floor, allowing Alexander and the girls to tickle him.

As for myself, I finally decided to follow my heart—I have begun my own mural business. By word of mouth (and an article published in the Post) I have become quite busy as a commissioned muralist specializing in trompe l'oeil painting. My goal is to transform my clients' ideas into fine art on their walls, furniture, etc., in homes, restaurants, and businesses. Will and the kids are so understanding of my need to be continuously creating; my family accepts the pitfalls of an artist/mother's temperament. Neither the kids nor Will know what they might find me making at any given time on any given day! They do, however, know that they will meet their early demise if they mess with my paint and brushes...

Well, there you have it: a mixture of pure bedlam, the city zoo, laundromat, and cafeteria, and a house forever meant to be *hopping—finally at one permanent location. If we keep all that we have been blessed with, we are most fortunate indeed! And so, from all of us to you, we extend our dearest hopes that this year will provide you the balance and yearning to embrace your journey.*

Wishing you warm winter nights and a heartfelt holiday season!

With love, Will, Dana, Scott, Robert, Alexander, Jennifer and Nicole Andrews

CHAPTER 6

Finding My Voice

I remember hearing Glen Campbell on the radio when I was about ten years old. Something in the sound touched me, and from that moment I knew I had to learn to play the guitar. I took a few lessons, but really I taught myself how to play—with the countless hours I spent banished in my bedroom, I had plenty of opportunity to practice. It wasn't long before I started to write my own songs, needing to create what I'd yet to hear before. This became another powerful way to express my painful feelings.

By the time I was fourteen, I was performing on the local college coffeehouse circuit. I would play on weekend evenings at college campuses in the New England area. I would always tell my parents when and where I'd be performing, but they were not interested—they wouldn't even give me a ride to where I was performing. When I entered my college nursing program, I continued to perform there and at other area colleges.

On one particular Friday night, in my sophomore year, I was going to perform at my college. That weekend, my paternal grandfather was visiting with his second wife from the Midwest, and my parents decided to bring them to hear me perform. There was a nice turnout: about fifty people filled the space, a large multi-purpose area with tables and chairs, big potted plants, and a café serving coffee, tea, and desserts. As I played, I couldn't ignore my mother talking the entire time I sang. When I would announce the title of my next song and tell a little about it, Mother would then loudly interject, asking me who the song was about, or when or why I wrote it. Inappropriate again, she was trying to control the situation—she just couldn't stay in the background and let me perform. As much as I wanted to ignore her, I simply couldn't—she would have never forgiven me. I'd be ridiculed and resented for years to come.

Making my way down my playlist, I came to a song that she had actually inspired. "Get Out of My Life" had practically written itself, taking me maybe ten minutes to compose. I simply announced the name of the song. Immediately she stood up and started waving her hands in the air, proclaiming excitedly, "It's about ME! This is MY song!" This meant that she managed not to hear the words I was singing. There she stood, trying desperately to make eye contact with anyone she could, so she could share her excitement. She was so trapped inside her own bubble that she couldn't process how this song addressed the mess she had made of my childhood and teenage years. Other people noticed her behavior—how could they not?—but tried to ignore her. My father was powerless to say anything.

It was a surreal moment. But by then I felt that I was over her craziness, and I kept focused on my friends who were there. I wasn't nervous. I knew my songs came from a place of truth. She couldn't stop me from crafting the stories written by my soul, or from sharing them with others.

I've continued to write songs that deal with intense experiences—either of my own or stories that have moved me. Many of the thirty-plus songs I've written tell stories of people I've known, friends who have died, and of events that have touched me deeply, including my pregnancies. By now, I know when there is a song brewing inside me. I will walk around for days, feeling like there is something I need to say, but I can't quite capture. It's like I'm constantly carrying a heavy bag that I cannot put down. Suddenly I find myself picking up my guitar, and the tune and lyrics just flow. At that point, they will not be stopped. If I am not near my guitar or piano, I will be singing them in my head. Most of my songs are not happy songs; it's as though it was the sadness that I needed to get out and let go. The happiness is something that is a work in progress.

Writing songs, I know, is part of a continuum of creative expression that began when I was just a little girl. I always had a desire to make things myself, starting with my first drawings. And I've learned, just as when I heard that Glen Campbell song on the radio, that sometimes I will be struck by a desire to do something new, something that speaks to me loud and clear—and when that happens, I cannot ignore it.

Growing up, I taught myself how to make lots of different things. I was good with my hands, and I had to make do with very little. The feeling of being able to make something for myself was very empowering. I figured out how to sew, how to knit sweaters, how to make macramé plant hangers. It was a way to give myself some of the things I wanted that I had been deprived of. This habit of doing for myself continued, and when I started earning money from babysitting, I would buy what I couldn't make. In my senior year of high school, looking forward to going to the prom with Will, I asked Mother if we could go out to buy me a dress. Her answer was priceless: "Why on earth would I buy you anything, especially a dress?" I wasted no time. I used my babysitting money and walked to a thrift shop about three miles away. I found a beautiful wedding gown for twenty-five dollars. I loved it, and I never thought twice about buying it. I did wish I could have had my hair and makeup done like the rest of my friends did, and I hoped that someday I would be able to do that for my daughters. Thankfully, that wish has come true.

Feeling constantly squelched, belittled, and undermined as a child can cause a multitude of unfortunate consequences. It can turn someone into a cold, bitter soul who never wants children because of their own disastrous childhood. It can result in parents who continue this same abusive behavior with their own children. In my case, thankfully, I was able to draw on my inner well to keep my emotions from turning bitter.

Usually, once I was alone in my room after weathering another storm of emotion from my mother, my tears would dry, and I would experience a fresh burst of life—some special resilience coming from deep inside. It would always come in the form of a new project I would explore, whether in painting, drawing, sewing, or music.

At first, the songs I wrote mostly concerned my aspirations and dreams, while later they became more introspective, and expanded to include others' situations and world events. I would hear about a tragedy from somewhere faraway that would grab me and not let go, until I would write a song about it. I often wonder if my concern for others' situations made it easier to not focus on mine.

Flight 800 is a song I wrote about a plane crash off the coast of New York City. I remember hearing a father being interviewed about his daughter, who died on that flight. He continued to ask himself if he had told her he loved her enough. His deep regret stayed with me, pushing me to write the song.

Flight 800

We look back to find the days that we remember.
They've run away with time, where was I?
I can still hear your baby cry, I rocked you.
I watched you fall asleep, I kissed your tiny feet,
And I shared your dreams.

Together we learned with pain comes laughter.
So many things to do, so many games to play.
The beauty of each day, just like a candle,
Melted away, just like chalk pictures that we made after a spring rain

Did I tell her I loved her enough?
I'd do anything to tell her once more.
The magic of her spirit keeps me warm at night.
The brightest star gives the most light

The journey of a lifetime it was meant to be.
Soon the bird in flight fell to the sea.
Sinking to the ocean floor, silent forever more
Bits of debris are all that's left of her for me.

You were too young to understand some answers
Could not be understood, and all the things that should have been
You never had the chance to go to France.
To marry and have kids, all the things you never did.
I ask God why?

Did I tell you I loved you enough?
I'd do anything to tell you once more.
The magic of your spirit keeps me warm at night.
The brightest star gives the most light

One of my songs, "Torch the Dawn," tells the story of an Israeli woman who takes her children on a bus, which is blown up by a suicide bomber. In this song I integrated the horror I felt when hearing of this heinous tragedy, and the unimaginable heartache with its long-term effects on the people on both sides of the conflict.

Torch the Dawn

She rode along. Her kids in tow,
hoping to go for a ride.
Immersed in song, too busy to know
There'd soon be nowhere to hide

The fire rages on
To torch the dawn
Children will die in their mothers' arms.
Rise with your son.
He'll carry your gun,
And learn to kill children like you once bore.
You'll teach him to maim in the face of war.

The saddest part that breaks my heart
Is how helpless she must have felt.
To help them grow, and then watch them die,
This is the greatest of sins

The fire rages on to kill the dawn
Children will die in their mothers' arms.
Oh, can't you see we're no closer to peace?
When will the gunfire from battle cease?
When will the wounds of war heal?

So still they lay, in their family grave,
too young to be so brave.
A land so strong, do fight as long as you can.
You might die, but you'll still belong.

The fire rages on
To torch the dawn
Children will die in their mothers' arms.
Rise with your son.
He'll carry your gun,
And learn to kill children like you once bore.
How many deaths can we still ignore?

My songwriting is still a mystery to me; I only know that throughout the tumultuous years of my growing up, when I felt constantly under assault, the music became a cornerstone of my self-preservation. I wrote the song, "Nineteen Years," after waking up from a dream about my parents dying in a car crash. I remember thinking at first how for nineteen years of my life, I had assumed each day they would wake up to see who I was. Although they were abusive and unloving, they were the only parents I had ever known. As I sat to let these feelings out, the irony flowed: for nineteen years I had been waiting for them to see me, they had not. Instead, for nineteen years they invalidated, chastised, degraded, and undermined me.

Nineteen Years
The tears, they dry on my eyelids at night, come morning I'll
dry them.
You'd do the same if you knew what I'd been through.
I'll never forget them.

For nineteen years I assumed they'd awaken,
but now I find they are gone.
For the rest of my life I'll spend torn up and shaken
and my blinds will be drawn.

Feelings of anger, pain and regret,
I could have done more. Some things they did and some things
they said,
I couldn't ignore.

For nineteen years I assumed they'd awaken,
but now I find they are gone.
For the rest of my life I'll spend torn up and shaken
and my blinds will be drawn.

Living alone in the darkness, I wonder,
can I hear them sleeping?
Living a life in a world torn asunder,
again I am weeping.

For nineteen years I assumed they'd awaken,
but now I find they are gone.
For the rest of my life I'll spend torn up and shaken
and my blinds will be drawn.

For many years after that, my blinds would remain drawn.

Another song I wrote, "You Couldn't Save the Life You Made," was written after the birth of Nicole, our fifth child. As I held her in my arms immediately after her birth, I was struck by how incredibly precious her little life was. In this healing moment, I celebrated God's fulfilling His end of our pact. He had given me a fifth chance to undo the disastrous childhood I'd endured. Still, in this song of joy, I looked back to address my mother.

You Couldn't Save the Life You Made
This was to be a song of love,
the generations growing up.
Mothers to daughters, sons of fathers;
the age-old recipe for time.

I was the child you gave birth to.
And now a woman set free.
You never knew how to love me.
This heart will mend again.
The loss within me still remains.
I'll learn to deal with this pain.
The years will bring me
new songs to sing.
The loves I have will never fade.
Forever after
it will not matter.
You couldn't save the life you made.

The songs I write these days are mostly happy ones—I feel I have so much to celebrate. I have written Will three Valentine's Day songs, a birthday song, and several songs for our children. I also have more time now, and the creativity comes in numerous forms, music only being one of them. I wake up each day, letting my soul dictate the best vehicle for the message that needs embodiment. It really doesn't matter whether it takes the form of a song, a painting, a poem, or a mural, because they are all sweet celebrations of my survival. I hope they can talk to your experiences, trials, and eventual survival and triumph, too.

December 2000

Greetings!

Today began as a more or less typical day... Kids oversleeping, spilled orange juice on the kitchen floor, my flight from the shower to the front door with wet hair and no coat, as we make our mad dash to the bus stop... Always I am overcome with relief once all five kids are school-bound! But for some reason, instead of hurrying home this morning, I stood still. I became unaware of the passing cars, the laundry list of chores awaiting me, and my dripping, wet curls, which were now frozen.

It seems I was frozen. On this frosty, wintry morning I surrendered to an unmet need for... today. Although last night has become a part of yesterday, whatever happened to today? In our preoccupation with political rubble, imminent deadlines, and holiday madness, we lose sight of all we really have—this day. This reality—the present—is really such a long-lost gift!

On this day, my view changed from that of a telescope to a microscope. Beyond the beauty of bare branches, which allow us a better view of the crisp winter sky, I realized the magnitude of my gratefulness for all parts of this day, especially my family and friends.

This past year has brought an abundance of both. Within the walls of this old farmhouse echoes a concerto: in this case, the instruments yield laughter, teasing, screaming, and more. In retrospect, I can honestly say that we enjoyed Robert's seventeen-boy sleepovers, the surprise dinner guests (consisting of six hungry teenagers), and late-night band practices sometimes lasting two days. These and other events from this past year lend a healthy balance towards the perspective of today. Maintaining this balancing act is the only consistency with this family of seven. Actually, we are really just a three-ring circus on most days!

Scott, who sees himself as the ringleader, is now fifteen, a junior in high school, as well as an officer in his youth group. Inside of that handsome, five-foot, ten-inch guy is a sports-loving, kind-hearted, awesome human being. He makes it a priority to donate a portion of his weekly allowance to an organization that feeds hungry children in third-world countries. He also enjoys writing computer programs, playing games, and occasionally doing some homework. This sweet guy inherited Will's math skills, which come in handy when his siblings need assistance with math homework. When our plans for him do not involve emptying the kitchen trash or sharing anything other than homework help with his siblings, Scott is completely content.

Rapping and drumming in his bedroom-turned-studio is thirteen-year-old eighth-grader, Robert. This past May he became a Bar Mitzvah, and it was a blessed event for us all. In early September, I got to know Robert's new teachers especially well; several times weekly they would call me to complain about his antics. It seems that he felt their classroom was the perfect stage for his acting. They were trying to teach the class about the Civil War, while he tried to reenact it! At the same time, Robert would come home each day and beg us to take him to audition for acting. We decided to take him for some auditions, and we were totally surprised when he acquired an agent/manager, then soon after landed several roles in commercials and came in second for a lead role in a film starring Anthony Hopkins. Underneath the humor lies a teenager with immeasurable sensitivity, creativity, and zest for living!

Never reaching satiation in his quest for knowledge is ten-year-old Alexander, who devours books with lightning speed. Alexander is enjoying fifth grade—but the real challenge for him comes in the form of video games, for which he has a passion that rivals none. He possesses a respect and quest for justice, which render him sensitive to others' needs and situations. When he overhears a quarrel between his sisters, after listening to both sides of their stories, he will play arbitrator and impart his wisdom. When his sisters are not content with his verdict, he tells them, "This case is closed! You both wanna take this to Daddy when he gets home? You'll really be sorry then!" One day he enlightened me to the fact that not everyone can excel in math, but that when it comes to matters of the heart, I rule!

Jennifer, almost nine, enjoys third grade tremendously. She has made many new friends both from school and also her softball and soccer teams. Although Jennifer resembles me, her personality is that of Will's—behind her contagious smile is a warm, fuzzy heart! She is a splendid combination of sensitivity and practicality. While she has no interest in playing house with Nicole, she seems to understand that Nicole still loves playing this familiar game. Jennifer recently revealed her plan; "I will play house with Nicole only if she will be the baby and I am the older sister who gets to boss her around." Long gone are the days of playing with Bucket Head, her beloved doll; reading on her bed and sleepovers with friends are her current rage. Best of all are the tender hugs she bestows upon us nightly, announcing, "It's snuggle time, guys!" This is the "food" that sustains my heart and soul...

And what would a holiday letter be without Nicole? What would our house be like without Nicole (a.k.a., Miss Spitfire)? Quieter, neater, more sane, but so very boring! Now seven, this second grader loves pizza, Britney Spears, candy, anything pink or purple, cheerleading, dance class, and her best little buddy Luke, who has Down's syndrome. It warms my heart to see her bonding with this adorable ten-year-old with Harry Potter glasses and a blond bowl haircut. She finds a way to include him in everything she can; together they watch cartoons, and little Luke will stay for dinner. Nicole told me that "Luke might not be tall, and he talks differently, but his heart is loving, and one day soon he will catch up to everyone else." After our nightly snuggle, Nicole is the first one fast asleep, holding onto her best loves—Mabel and Bunny. (Her other stuffed pig, Winchester, "likes to live on a shelf in the closet because he got shy.")

Will, the saint of the family, gets home just in time to savor the after-school cyclone and impending comedy hour/food fight and, at times, barbaric dinner show! Unequivocally Will is the glue that holds our family together and me intact. His devotion to his profession, along with research and mentoring medical students and residents, is second only to his devotion to his family. Ever patient, he always has a listening ear, an understanding nature, and the most hopeful of hearts.

Me… I continue to be lost in the laundry of life, forever searching for that lost sock (or is it my lost sanity?). With the December chill, I have given myself permission to resume my winter hobbies. This is the time I long for all year: bread baking, soup making, quilting, wool spinning. I continue to paint murals, but decided to focus more on volunteering. I have become the Brownie Leader for 19 girls at our girls' elementary school. Between our smiles and luscious Girl Scout cookies, together we will make our community a better place! Mostly, I try to be everything I can for my family and friends. I focus on helping our children understand that we are all but a tiny part of a huge plan.

As the holidays approach, and the New Year rounds the corner, freeze today as the greatest gift we have. Even if for one short moment, stop to listen to the winter birds sing, the winds whistle, and the magical, yet barely audible, sound of snowflakes making their feather-like descent. If you stop for long enough, you will see how each unique snowflake contributes toward a soft blanket; so fragile that it can be enjoyed for only a short time. We are each a unique snowflake contributing towards the whole of mankind. All that we have to offer is ourselves, today.

Finally, this brings us to you, always in our thoughts throughout the year, not just at holiday time, when Hallmark moments rule. From our hearts to yours, we wish you a happy, healthy 365 days, each filled with all the hope, kindness, giving, and love your little soul can muster!

Happy Holidays with love,
Will, Dana, Scott, Robert, Alexander, Jennifer and Nicole Andrews

CHAPTER 7

Terrible Teens

My transition to becoming a teenager was difficult at best. I was observant enough to see that my friends were earning more autonomy and respect in their families, while I received less and less. Whenever I would assert myself, I was met with punishments and ridicule. Any expression of my changing self was squashed. Once at the dinner table, my mother brought up the name of a boy at school. I commented, "He's such a stud!" Immediately my father harshly interjected, "Don't you *ever* use that term again! A stud is a male horse! You are so stupid; you use words you don't even know the meaning of. *Think* before you open your mouth. Get out of here, and go to your room!"

One summer, Mother and I went swimming at a neighbor's pool. I was twelve then. Mother looked at my legs and accused me of shaving them. I hadn't. My neighbor interceded, telling mother I was a young lady and should be allowed to shave my legs. Needless to say, my mother hated this neighbor from that day on. Later, when I ventured to shave my legs, trim my own hair, or lighten it in the summertime, my actions were met with severe punishments.

When I got my period at the age of thirteen, my mother was furious. Bianca still hadn't begun menstruating, and soon after, Mother began taking her from one doctor to another to understand why. In contrast, she couldn't be bothered to deal with my first period directly—she made my father go to the pharmacy to buy me sanitary napkins. He then came to me holding out a paper bag and told me, "I am so proud of you. Use these wisely." His words confused me. At thirteen I couldn't say exactly why this interaction was wrong, even bizarre, but it made me incredibly uncomfortable.

In short, my becoming an adolescent freaked Mother out. Things weren't helped by the fact that I had begun receiving attention from boys—unlike Bianca, who by then was very overweight. Sometimes, when Bianca found a boy to come over to our house, he would end up calling me. After that, I was made to stay in my room when she invited someone over. Basically, Mother was completely unable to separate her own irrational fears from me and my life. In her eyes, I was always on the verge of having sex; she would warn me, "Bells don't ring when you have sex." She said that if I were wearing a bathing suit and was near a boy, it was the same as being naked. She was also terrified of driving on the highway, and she told me I should be, too.

My mind and conscience were in constant battle. While I knew mother was wrong in not allowing me autonomy, I had to learn to be sneaky at times when I knew things were within my rights to do. These ranged from small things like trimming my hair to make bangs, or lightening my hair with peroxide, to going out on dates with boys who weren't Jewish. I believed I was inherently good, in that I never did anything I would regret or be ashamed of; sadly, the simple act of being my own person constituted a transgression. The more Mother punished, the more I resisted. I became steadfast in reaching for what should have been mine. Even as the punishments continued, and Mother and Bianca did whatever they could to shut me down, I just knew I wasn't going to give up. When the punishment was already as bad as it could get, I would speak my mind. But it all took a toll: while my resolve and tenacity strengthened, my self-esteem plummeted.

During this time, Mother often reminisced about the sweet and docile baby I had been. Maybe my being such an undemanding child had led her to her believe I would always be quiet and never present any challenge for her. What a shame I had grown to become inconvenient, a nuisance, and "the bane of her existence."

When I was in my freshman year of high school, I started keeping a diary. I would write in it when I was sad, hurting, or angry. I added to it weekly, sometimes several times in one week, "telling" my diary about boys, school, and mostly about my parents or sister. It was a sanctuary for me, a place to vent over my continuous violations and hurts. There was no one else in my life who could "hear me out" like this.

It wasn't until later, when I started dating Will, that I felt there was a real person I could reveal myself to in this way. It was my sweet Will who helped me begin to stand up for my right to own myself. He loved me enough to believe that I could be whole once I walked away. He not only saw me for who I was and could become, he instantly saw through my mother. Of course, this meant my mother saw him as a threat to her hold over me. On several occasions, my parents wrote letters to Will, telling him they thought I was on drugs; they went on to assert that since my behavior toward them was so awful, I would end up treating him horribly too.

The summer after my junior year, I got a job working as a day camp counselor. I always loved to surround myself with kids; they speak what their heart knows. Sure, they can be mean. They can tease. But they can also show us a fresh point of view and a surprising new perspective. For me, this summer job was also a chance to see how kids with loving parents lived. I wanted to live a normal childhood—even just one summer of a normal childhood, even vicariously—through these lucky, loved children. When their moms picked them up at carpool, I could see and hear their dogs barking excitedly, greeting the kids from the backs of their moms' station wagons. They had dogs! When I escorted them into their cars, their moms would smile and ask how their days at camp had been. Their moms cared! As I watched them leave to go home, my dreams went with them, sitting in the back seat right next to them and their happy dogs.

Each afternoon my heart filled with an escalating dread, which lasted until I got into my mother's car and gained a sense for how *her* day had gone. If it was a good day, and no one had made her angry, it would be a good day for me, as long as I didn't do anything to anger her. If, however, her day was not good, I could take care of everything. I was her scapegoat. We no longer had a dog for her to smack with a rolled-up newspaper, so I was next in line…

It was one of the hottest days of the year: ninety-six degrees, scorching, and humid. Breathing the air was like trying to inhale soup. I looked forward to going home, since our house was, thankfully, air-conditioned. On this day, however, that wouldn't matter. That was the last place I'd ever want to be... again. As I got in the car, I saw my mother was crying. She wept for the entire ride home. I asked her what was wrong, but she continued to weep, unable to answer my repeated questions.

For me, the pain got exponentially worse. I knew I was in trouble and would have hell to pay for something, but I had no idea for what. When we got home she finally spoke: she directed me to go to my room, and not come out until my father came home. Oh, boy. How do you do something *that bad*, yet have *no clue* as to what? I lay on my bed wondering what I had done, what my punishment would be, and if this time she would allow my father to have any mercy on me.

When I heard a knock on the door, it was actually a relief. There stood my father, telling me a talk was in order. He came into my room and sat at my desk. I sat on my bed. Then he slapped something down onto my desk. I recognized it immediately... my diary. *My diary!*

I wished that my mother hadn't rifled through my room. I wished I had hidden my diary in a safer place. I wished I were anywhere but there. I wished I were dead...

My father calmly opened my diary. He proceeded to read line after line out loud, while I felt my soul being torn apart piece by piece. He would stop after almost every line, either to rant about how wrong I was, or to ask an incriminating question and then force me to answer it. When I remained silent, he spat in my face and screamed, "*Answer me, little girl!*" I was sixteen. I was no longer a little girl. To him and to mother, I was... a little nothing, a nuisance that they could crush under their shoe. As he went on, my body felt cold, my tongue was paralyzed. I wanted to scream at him, "*This is mine!*" He was a child psychiatrist, trained to help children and young people! How could he not know how devastating it would feel to be violated by hearing your own written words being read back to you, by your *own father*? The anguish was unbearable. These were my innermost thoughts! Before my eyes, he turned it all—my private thoughts, poetry, dreams, all my hurt feelings and anger, and everything else written in my precious diary—into a weapon, and then he turned it on me. My diary, my trusted confidant, was turned against me. I felt as if I had been turned inside out. Nothing would be safe anymore, ever again. Not my parents, not my diary, not my heart.

Sadly, that day I lost all respect for my father. He did something that went beyond the boundaries that any loving parent should respect. Mother forced him to do this, but he had gone along. Mother knew she had won, and she wasted no time sharing all the details with her friends and relatives: not only of the discovery, and my father's punishing behavior, but of what I said in my diary. I cannot find a way to ever forget or forgive them for taking away the one thing I had found to trust in—my diary. But my father should have known better. This was not ok and never will be. To this day I cannot visit his grave.

Yet, as time went on, and I had children of my own, I continued to crave his love. I always knew deep down that he could have and would have been a kindhearted man if not for mother and Bianca. It would be many years—until he was on his deathbed—before I could achieve some measure of peace with my father.

December 2001

Greetings to you and yours!

There is no more perfect a day than this to begin writing my favorite letter of the year—this, to you! Looking out the second floor window on this mild winter day grants all the inspiration I need. The afternoon sun has cast an orange haze upon the bare tree branches; to me these branches look like arms reaching to the powers that be to find all the hope and healing we sorely need. Our thoughts and prayers rest with the souls of those tragically lost this past September 11th.

The holiday feeling arrived in our household early this year. The kitchen is garnished in grapevine garland dressed with cinnamon sticks, gingerbread men and cookie cutters, pinecones, winter berries, small wooden spoons, and gingham bows. The rest of our house is decorated in a theme appropriate for all seasons: clutter, ceaseless chaos, cackling, and five cavorting children!

The oldest of these would be sixteen-year-old Scott. We really look up to him; he's almost six feet tall! A senior in high school, Scott now has his driving permit. This year he built another computer from scratch, and this comes in handy for his new web design and consulting business, XLR8. Fortunately his grades are excellent; otherwise Scott's business will be renamed DCLR8. Scott's many interests include tutoring his girlfriend in math, playing roller hockey and touch football, his youth organization, electric guitar, and cooking. You might be curious as to what "cooking" would consist of; that would be anything that involves eggs, cheese, and various other ingredients meeting his approval for his own consumption.

I have come to believe that fourteen-year-old Robert knows no other way of living than this: a world including a lifetime supply of candy, eBay transactions, drumming for his band, playing guitar, piano by ear, and eating lemon squares and pumpkin pie. Robert will tell you he practices best between the hours of ten p.m. until whenever we are trying to sleep. In the summertime and on weekends we paint murals alongside one another. When not painting, Robert is making and selling embroidered patches on eBay, after teaching himself how to use my embroidering machine! I tell him that my grandpa is smiling in heaven; Robert and I are the only ones in our family who inherited our sewing aptness from this highly skilled tailor.

The business at hand in eleven-year-old Alexander's world involves a vast array of computer games, where he needs only touch a key to fend off evil villains. To the dismay of his siblings, Alexander has become even more skilled at rhyming—when the dinner table discussion turns to school, he quips, "Top notch day, got an A, Nicole, your pigs get in my way, I'll sell them on eBay..." and more. Because he is so quiet you might not be aware of his profound sense of justice, sensitivity to animals, and ability to comprehend others' circumstances. When we moved to this house, we were entrusted with the care of the outdoor cat the owners could not take with them. When Buddy passed away, it was Alexander who insisted we contact the previous owner to invite them to Buddy's "funeral." He wrote a little eulogy, and he even drew Buddy's name on a rock.

Nine-year-old Jennifer loves reading, learning violin, riding her bike, rollerblading, and playing soccer, softball, and hockey. Not only is Jennifer unconcerned that she is the sole girl on the hockey team, but she had never played a day of hockey in her life when she entered the rink for tryouts. Like Will, Jennifer possesses a level perspective. When asked if she was nervous about being the first female on her team, she responded, "When I help my team to win, no one will care whether I am a boy or girl!" Recently, she found out that her best friend would be moving far away. Jennifer promised her friend that if she ever decides to run away from home, this friend's house would be her intended destination.

The violins sound whenever eight-year-old Nicole makes her grand entrance. She loves to make greeting cards from magazines, and she adores fashioning her own belts out of Will's discarded neckties. She enjoys dance classes, and she often entertains Will when he comes home *from work. In her ballet attire, she patiently waits by the kitchen door for him to walk in. She takes a running leap into his arms, and this little ballerina wins her daddy's heart every time. On many nights, Will takes a back seat to her beloved piggies, even though their pink fur is mostly loved off by now. I am convinced Nicole is a very old soul; she is simply too comfortable in her own life to have not been here before.*

Always so giving of his time, his love, and his paycheck, Will makes sure his family wants for nothing. His priority is clearly his family; he assists the kids with their homework and school projects, assumes much of the driving to Hebrew School and sporting events, and manages to be there for each of us in so many ways. One of the sweetest perks of his professional life is the yearly meetings he attends, and the destinations make for wonderful family vacations, or sometimes, romantic getaways for the two of us. Will has always had an avid interest in reading fantasy and science fiction, and he collects medieval armor and weaponry. He is absolutely over the moon at the release of "Lord of the Rings"...

As for me, I continue to run on fumes, and I ride faster than the witch in the "Wizard of Oz"—most of the time I feel like I am the cyclone! (On occasion, our children would suggest I am the witch.) I continue to be the Brownie leader for twelve spunky, adorable little girls. Together we bake cookies, learn how to help in family chores, spent a month making a quilt for a little girl who has Rett Syndrome, and made posters to cheer our soldiers in Afghanistan. My mural business has really picked up, and somehow I manage to make time for sewing, knitting, and spinning wool. I have been doing more oil painting, which fills my soul to the very brim.

Things continue to hop at the Andrews household! Actually, they more likely scurry about and are covered in warm hamster fur. The hamsters made their debut at Chanukah, but they had best live on forever, or risk breaking Alexander, Jennifer, and Nicole's hearts. I told Will these hamsters are pretty observant little creatures; they watch me buzz around the house all day long, then fly 'round their wheel, doing their Dana impression...

We have all learned so much, yet hurt so deeply this past fall. Like wounded children, we need Band-Aids for our souls. Having chosen to gain my American Citizenship now seems so much more meaningful to me. One thing is certain; we are strong and we will endure. We may never realize how many lives we can touch in any one noble moment; it is our wish for you that this coming year will afford you numerous chances to reach deeply into as many hearts as you are able!

Especially throughout this New Year, we will keep you in our warmest, gentlest thoughts and prayers. May this coming year bring good health, much comfort for our tenderhearted souls, success in all you endeavor, and most importantly, loud laughter from floor to rafters!!!

From our seven hearts to yours, happy holidays and a blessed New Year!

All our love, Will, Dana, Scott, Robert, Alexander, Jennifer and Nicole Andrews

CHAPTER 8

Getting Out

I was desperate, and I was always searching for others who could give me the support I so desperately needed. Many of my friends' parents were horrified to see my mother's heinous behavior towards me. But they did not step in. They knew the repercussions that would follow from challenging her and violating her rules. They saw how far she went with me.

When I was fifteen, I had a babysitting job for a couple with two children. One day, the mom remarked to me how proud my mother must be, to have such a sweet and responsible daughter. That opened a door that I was determined to walk right through! I began telling her everything. This woman reacted with shock and anger. She called Mother, and she told her she could not ignore what she was hearing and had to speak up. My mother, of course, told her that I had been lying—and that she should never have trusted me with her children in the first place.

When I came home later that day, mother sat me down and lectured—actually, screamed—at me for over an hour. She accused me of telling "unmitigated lies," and she insisted that I had no business talking to anyone outside of our family about what went on in our house. (Funny how she never had the slightest problem informing others about my behavior.) As she warmed up, she reminded me that I should always remember I was a mistake; things would have been better if they *had* aborted me. She then suggested I tell Will about the lies I shared, and that I let him know he deserves so much better than me. When he came to visit me that afternoon, I sobbed as I told him I didn't deserve him and that he needed to find a better girlfriend. Sweet Will... My sweet, sweet Will grabbed my hand, took me out for ice cream, and listened as I cried my heart out. He then reassured me that he saw beyond my mother's antics. He always said he believed she was "empty" on the inside, always looking to others for drama and gossip.

Maybe because Mother felt so threatened by my small steps toward autonomy, my life at home continued to be hellish. When I was sixteen, things came to a head. I realized that it was me or them. I could not go on with the constant belittling, humiliation, and punishments I had endured for at least twelve of my sixteen years. Why did I have to continue? I had never done anything unlawful, and I only wanted my mother to love me (if that was not too much to ask). Each night I would lie in bed and beg God for just *one* day of happiness. What would that even be like? Did it really even exist? No human being should be treated like this, and denied the simple craving to feel good, worthy, and loved.

In my high school art class I had met a friend, Suzanne. Though she was also just sixteen, she was already married, to a twenty-seven-year-old man from her church. She came from an abusive situation as well. I shared my circumstances with her, and she shared with me the abusive experiences she had suffered with her own mother. Suzanne, who had escaped her situation by getting married, pointed out that I did not have to be subject to my parents' cruel behavior. I knew I was sick and tired of the incessant humiliation I endured. I also knew that things weren't ever going to change at home. I told Suzanne I had nowhere else to go. Mother had informed my grandparents, and all my other relatives, that I was an ungrateful and ignorant child, a bad seed, and trouble all around. She suggested I was spreading lies, and they should not get sucked into my stories about her. She then threatened that if they spoke to me, she would never speak to them again.

Suzanne invited me to move in with her and her husband, for fifty dollars a month. That night I packed my things to move out, putting my possessions into garbage bags. Going through my belongings was painful; too many years of pain and too many belongings to remind me of them. Sadly, not one of these belongings could sustain me in this hell. I would take along my houseplants, my guitar, paints, and the most important thing—what was left of my sanity. While I was packing, my father came into my room and spat in my face. He told me to "stop making so much *fucking* noise. No one wants you anyway, so you are wasting your time thinking you are welcome anywhere."

I moved out the next morning. Will had encouraged me in my decision to leave. He agreed to pick me up and drive me, with my worldly belongings, over to Suzanne's. Seeing us loading the car, my parents realized that I was really leaving.

My mother's next move spoke volumes. She grabbed her purse and car keys, and she announced, "I am going shopping." Sure enough, she drove off without so much as a wave. She was gone—taking with her all the nasty invasions and constant attacks on my soul, but also my hopes that one day *something* might finally trigger loving emotions from her. I realized I never had lived in her heart. Not many others ever did. Mother's heart was too small and cramped to admit all three of her children.

My father came up to me, and our eyes met. Seeing me about to leave had softened him: with tears in his eyes, he reached out to hold me. We both cried. I will never forget what he said then: "It can be so hard to grow up." It can be even harder to grow up in *this* household, I thought. And he had made it especially difficult because, out of his own fear of my mother's wrath, he never stood in her way. Somehow when she put her foot down, his psychiatric training vanished. He saved himself from her, but he couldn't save me. I often wonder if, instead, he *chose* not to save me.

During the time I lived with my friend, I wrote a lot of poetry. The first morning, I woke up to see it was gray and rainy outside. Sitting up in bed, I realized that it might be raining on the outside—but not inside my soul. It was gray outside, but surely the sun would come out again. I was free from the darkness that was my life at home. I reached for a pen, and I quickly wrote this poem on a still unpacked cardboard box:

How

How
could this heart hold so much pain?
More pain, it felt, than there are children in the world.
How
could your blind eyes and weak mind crush such a perfect little
bud?

How

do I stand after each fall, and then find my way back to you for
more?

How

can I ever learn to heal knowing that you cannot—but try to
love you still?

How

can you look and smell like mother, but swallow me like a lion
and scar me like an iron?

How

can I learn to love myself enough to lose the numbing pain and
feel myself breathe again?

I found a job downtown, and I skipped school every Friday to work as a secretary at an employment agency. This enabled me to pay rent and also have spending money. I continued to babysit on weekends to make ends meet. Suzanne was extremely mature for sixteen. She was kind and understanding. She and Will got along well, which I took as a good sign. Suzanne was one of the only people I've ever known who could stand up to my mother. When Mother called to speak to me, Suzanne had a conversation with her—and she put Mother in her place. Mother ended up calling me back and promising me things would be different if I came home. It was a promise I had yearned to hear for years. What I didn't realize at the time was that my mother was unwilling to lose her power over me—and certainly not to a sixteen year old. She had another opportunity to lure me back and, at the same time, reaffirm my need for her love and acceptance. Mother pulled out all the stops. In her usual manipulative way, she got her friends and some relatives to call me, telling me I was in the wrong, and I should give in and go home.

This did not sway me, though it wasn't easy to hear. Yet, even as I cherished my new freedom, other issues were cropping up. Suzanne and her husband began trying to get me to go to church with them every Sunday. I was too torn and uncertain about so many areas of my inner life; but Suzanne started pushing me to embrace her beliefs. My experience with religion up to that point was very inconsistent and tied up with my mother's extreme manipulativeness. Mother always told me I was not ever to talk back, meaning to disagree with her, because, as she said, "You only have one mother and one father. You are violating the commandments. You should go to hell for that." Then, there had been my parents' offer of a "choice" between having a Bat Mitzvah or a cruise. What kind of choice was that? My brother ended up getting both, of course.

The religious pressure from Suzanne only added to the pressure from school. Even though I kept up with my homework and studies well enough to make honor roll, someone at school noticed I was absent every Friday, when I went to work. My mother received a call from my school. She called Suzanne— who made her cry by telling her that she didn't deserve my love. Later that night my father called me, no doubt under orders from Mother. He sweet-talked me, telling me that this was all a part of adolescence, and promising that if I came home, he would make sure I was treated with more understanding. He also promised that he and my mother would pay for college—if I kept living at home and not in a dorm. (Bianca, meanwhile, was attending the state university and living in a dormitory.)

I knew it was a chance I had to take. After six months of living independently, I moved back home.

The first few days after I came back, my dad was the one who mostly communicated with me. Mother had more important things to attend to— shopping and lunches with friends. My dad knew I craved his attention and acceptance and love. After all, he was, of both parents, the only one who occasionally showed me something like tenderness. Within one week, things fell apart. Mother and Bianca were sickened by my new, healthier relationship with my father. He began to take the heat. He caved in and went back to the old ways, playing backup to Mother and Bianca's sick maneuvers. At this point I didn't have much choice. My attempt at independence had brought complications I wasn't able to surmount, and I knew I had to stay at home if I wanted a college education. I would have to become stronger and find more ways to be more independent.

At this point I was ready to graduate. I started spending most of my time with Will, who had begun medical school and had his own apartment. Even though I still had to deal with the old crap at home, I felt I was over it. Moving in with Suzanne, and knowing I could take steps to help myself, had taught me some profound lessons. I learned that I did have worth, and that it is ok to run from a place that your soul tells you is toxic.

November 2002

An early holiday hello!

It is early morning, and through the gaps in the windows of this old house I can hear (and feel) the cold wind howling. The last of the autumn leaves have made their annual descent, our pumpkin still boasts his somewhat toothless grin, the kids continue to inhale their Halloween stash, and there you sit, wondering if I realize that it is still November—and not December yet. As for why this year's letter is so early, you can take your pick:

- *Even when early, our holiday letters serve multiple purposes! You can use the margins of these pages to jot down ideas for your holiday party menu and holiday gift list.*
- *George, our happy mailman, promised me that when mailed now, our letter is unlikely to be competing with Toys R Us and Target coupon circulars for space in your mailbox.*
- *Just imagine how much longer this letter might be if written one month later!*
- *I can finally boast about being early for something.*
- *I'm no fool! Writing this beats raking leaves any day.*

I must confess—my real reason for writing this early is quite simple; recent world events have taught us to feel passion for every day. Today feels just as promising as any day in December to write this letter.

This past year has been filled with events and milestones. The trunk of my car was full as well—with Scott's college-bound belongings. Scott took a huge leap to the campus of Boston College, where he majors in Computer Engineering. Our fears of sadness were unfounded; we are thrilled for him to be enthralled with college life. Scott's unequivocal affection for his girlfriend continues. When she entered our home, she also entered our hearts. We occasionally get to see Scott on

weekends—thank goodness for girlfriends who live close to home, ne-
cessitating visits from their heartsick boyfriends.

Still living at home is fifteen-year-old Robert. When weekend
evenings roll around, he gathers his cohorts and they take their
antics to the neighborhood supermarket. Behind the market they discovered a large uninterrupted wall—which is just perfect for view-
ing movies. They plug in a laptop computer and projector and watch
DVDs while relaxing on pillows in the back of a pick-up truck! One
scenario I can always count on is having this tenth grader's many
friends congregate here. I've learned to always prepare extra food,
assuming I'll never be forewarned when his performance includes
dinner for his fans and friends. When not building frames for his
latest paintings, drumming, or composing piano tunes, Robert is
making customers' days at the mailing store nearby, where he is
now employed. He still makes time for his greatest passion—acting.
Recently he acted in two commercials, and in early December he
begins his first movie role.

Onwards to the one who is notorious for skipping meals... twelve-
year-old Alexander, constantly pursuing new books to read. If he is
not with book in hand, we know we can find him facing a computer
monitor. He has made several good friends who share the same passion
for video games. Lately Alexander has developed a great fondness for
my brother; I wonder if it is coincidental that my brother has an X-Box
video game system. Alexander now has weekly lessons preparing him
for his Bar Mitzvah next March. Lately he has developed an uncanny
aptitude for writing poetry and fiction...

Armed with a huge heart reserved for all things she holds dear,
ten-year-old Jennifer has such ardor for so many things. Jennifer has
discovered the immediate joy of instant messaging on the computer with
all of her friends. Like Alexander, she loves to read, but she also finds
joy in riding her bike outside, participating in as many sports as she
can find, and snuggling with our numerous cherished pets. Recently she
seemed to feel burdened with the fact that Alexander never endeavored

to ride a bike. She made up her mind that she would teach him to ride a two-wheel bike within a single day. Somehow she coerced him outside and was successful! It was heartwarming to see how proud she was watching her brother riding effortlessly past us time after time. He thought it was a blast!

Fourth-grader Nicole is still a piece of work! Her daily arrival from school is celebrated with her favorite snack—steamed artichoke. Like a tropical storm, she gathers debris as she moves inland, leaving a trail of sneakers, socks, and half-eaten artichoke leaves. Nicole will dig, search, gather, and even appropriate any and all items necessary to bring her latest invention to fruition. She created a tiara fit for the Queen of England using pipe cleaners, tassels she cut off the dining room pillows, and gems torn off one of my grandmother's old purses (this little "Queen of England" almost died at my own hands...) Several months ago we took her to visit her aging great-grandmother. Nicole decided to bring this spunky woman her favorite, cherished Beanie Baby. Her great-grandmother graciously offered to return it, lest Nicole might soon be missing it. Nicole responded, "Nana! This is the season for giving, not taking back!"

Will was recently promoted to Associate Professor in his specialty. He finds academics both stimulating and rewarding, writing scientific papers and books, while teaching medical students and residents. It is most definitely Will who keeps this "dog and pony show" intact. While taking charge of Hebrew School carpooling and animal care, he keeps both the inside and outside of the house in check, and most importantly, he maintains the moral decorum. The kids and I have a tremendous respect for him; he embraces the best values with such conviction and devotion, all wrapped up in a blanket of dry-witted humor.

Emerging from a blanket of clean, yet-to-be-folded laundry you will find me, wearing one of my many hats. My favorite would be the striped one from "Cat in the Hat"—my plans are subject to numerous changes, and I must arm myself with plans A through Z! My outdoor murals on a children's playhouse won the Peoples' Choice Award, and I am creating murals for the library at our children's upper elementary school. I am extremely grateful for this artistic ability, and I never take it for granted. One recent evening, when Will came home to find me painting yet another mural, he declared, "I didn't buy us a house. I bought you an expensive canvas!" At one point I contemplated returning to nursing, but decided that my mural business provides me much more flexibility with the children's needs now.

Surely this year has been packed full of all colors in the spectrum. Still, through all the challenges, we built strength. This past August, Will's aunt succumbed to multiple sclerosis at age fifty-six. Although her loss was tragic, the service in her honor was very fitting for such a beautiful woman. We will surely miss her spunk and witty sense of humor.

Sadly, in July we lost our twenty-year-old cat, Ashley. She has been a part of Will and me since we got married. Then, we celebrated Alexander's graduation from the upper elementary school by adopting a cat for him. Timmy is a marmalade kitten with a face cuter than a bug's ear. In between catnaps, he spends his spare time chasing his tail. I can honestly say that he got that idea from me!

This past November, Will and I celebrated our twentieth wedding anniversary with an incredible trip to England. We stayed at both a castle and quaint bed and breakfasts, dined in pubs, went to museums, saw Big Ben, and were enamored of the small, sleepy towns where we stopped for tea and antique shopping.

As I write this holiday letter, I realize one thing: not only is the journey far more important than the destination, but the passion with which we "set sail" is the real crux of life. We learned that futures might fall in mid-flight, but thankfully, we have today to embrace with a full heart. We maintain a deep appreciation for every blessing, no matter how small.

May this coming winter find you nestled beneath warm blankets beside a roaring fire in the hearth. We wish you an endless supply of hot chocolate, good books, and an awesome outdoor view of scarf-adorned snowmen enjoying their glistening residence.

With loads of love from our passionate hearts to yours——Happy Holidays!

Will, Dana, Scott, Robert, Alexander, Jennifer, and Nicole Andrews

CHAPTER 9

Janine

Each fall, once the crisp "sweater days" come along, I think of my friend Janine. She was slight, had pretty, curly, dark-brown hair and huge, round, dark eyes, and boasted the sweetest smile I had ever seen. Always happy, she was never without a song to sing and the harmony to accompany it.

Janine and I had met through our synagogue youth group when we were both in ninth grade. Even though we attended different schools, we became fast friends, and we got together often. She could play anything on the piano, and I so admired her talent. More than her musical abilities, it was clear to me that she was extremely bright. I wished I were as smart as she was! Her parents were never home when I came over, just their housekeeper, who mostly spoke Spanish. Janine's home was always clean, but it lacked color and personality—just like her family. The few times I met her family, they were courteous, but offered no personality or emotion. They reminded me of robots. I vividly remember wanting to tell them a joke or tickle them, just to see if they *were* human and might respond! Janine was their exact opposite: just as intelligent, but musically gifted and a sensitive, artistic soul.

When her parents were around, Janine would avoid them. I often wondered why, and one day her reason became clear. As we sat together on the piano bench while she played her favorite classical music, she suddenly lifted her fingers from the keys and looked at me, her eyes welling with tears. In the sudden silence, seeing how upset she was, I reached to hug her.

"No," she said, pulling away from me. "Hugs can't fix this. I am so *mad*! I *hate* my father. He is an evil monster of a man. He cannot see me as a unique person. He will not allow me to choose any career but law. He already forced my mother and sister to go into law. I want music! I try to play and sing loudly when he comes home from work, but he shuts the kitchen door so he won't hear me. He has told me this is a done deal. *I hate that man!*"

I realized at that moment that we shared another bond besides our friendship and our love for music. We shared the travesty of parents who could only live within expectations as artificial and neat as a matching set of Tupperware containers. You could never mix and match items, because they were not interchangeable. There was no guesswork needed or new information allowed here. Why would you choose anything else? They couldn't fathom any reason for deviation.

My parents, especially my mother, had mastered the kind of emotionally abusive language that could overpower you and eat your heart out. Janine's parents were masters of deadly silence. We both continued to try harder: while I tried for my individual personhood to be seen and validated by my parents, she tried to be heard and accepted by hers. Mine were blind, and hers were deaf. We were both equally frustrated, angered, and crushed, and both of us hated our parents, feeling imprisoned within our lives even though we had committed no crime.

When it came time to go to college, we encountered more roadblocks. Janine wanted to pursue music; I wanted to study art. What we wanted was unfortunately not in keeping with our parents' desires and expectations. Janine's parents chose pre-law for her, and my parents chose nursing for me. Sadly, no matter how much she might have excelled at the career she wanted, she failed miserably at following the path her parents chose for her. I entered college, and somehow muddled along in the nursing program, feeling fortunate at least that I could minor in art. I was also lucky that Will, who by then was in medical school, was able to tutor me in my nursing courses.

But Janine had no boyfriend—no one to feed her a steady, sustaining diet of hope, to listen to her frustration and anger, to validate her inherent right to follow the aspirations dictated by her soul. During our freshman year, she began a downhill slide, which picked up speed with each skipped class, each written warning from puzzled professors, and each furious phone call from her angered parents. Janine was finally in charge, flying her own personal Kamikaze mission. By the end of the first semester, Janine had failed her courses. Her father pronounced her sentence: she would have to repeat them all in the spring.

With midterm exams looming, we didn't speak for several weeks. I didn't know that while I stayed up into the wee hours studying for my chemistry exam, Janine was pulling an all-nighter, too, her pen in hand, writing furiously. She finally had her chance to say all she wanted to, to tell her dad all he had refused to listen to. She would put in writing how he starved her every wish and dream, so he could read it—over and over again. Gathering up her courage, she placed the letter in an envelope and wrote his name on it. Now he could not deny who was the intended recipient and who was his victim.

Janine came home from college with the letter. Going quietly into her parents' bedroom, she looked through her father's closet until she found what she was looking for on the top shelf.

She dropped her note on the floor of the closet and put one bullet inside the chamber. She cradled his gun, knowing that it would end the pain that he inflicted. Ironically, she used *his* weapon to put an end to his sickening abuse. In the end, he finally gave his daughter what *she* wanted; a desperate, yet final, escape. One bullet was all she needed because she knew that this was one task she would get right the first time. She had one chance to make things right. Forever.

Concealing the gun inside one of her father's undershirts, she opened the door and left her house for the last time. Janine loved nature; she said it always freed her soul. Her soul now longed to be free. She let the shirt fall to the ground. I see her now: looking up to the sky, asking God to please take her to wherever good, kind, and loving souls journey. She took a deep breath through her nose, inhaling, for one last time, all the outdoor scents she wanted to bring with her. She loved the fall, and she could smell the last of the dried grass before the first frost. She was ready now. Ready to have the last word. The gun was in *her* hands. His gun. She cocked the gun and put it into her mouth. Blast. The single bullet tore through her brilliant brain, releasing exploded fragments of a beauteous life that would never ever be. All that was Janine was silenced, just like the silence she endured from her tormentor. Her plane went down long before it even executed a flight plan.

I was still living at home that semester, as my parents had insisted. One night, I returned home from a date with Will. When I passed my parents' bedroom, my mother called my name. I stopped at her door.

"Remember your friend Janine?" she asked. "Well, today she shot herself in the head and killed herself."

I froze, forgetting for a long moment how to breathe. Tears ran down my face. I remember needing a huge hug. This, of course, was not an option from my mother. Her idea of consolation? The realistic, yet cold, observation: "That's what happens in life. People die." What I would have given for a moment of compassion from her that night.

Several days later, surrounded by friends, we buried our friend. Despite the fact that her parents and the Rabbi made it seem that her life was taken by illness, we all knew the truth. Her loss was tragic and unnecessary. She had so many songs left to sing, so many hearts to touch.

I think about Janine now, and I imagine her life if she had lived. I wonder if, like me, she might somehow have dealt with her demons and ended up happily married with a family. I wonder if she would have the career in music she dreamed of. Sometimes, I wonder if she was born without that spark that can light the way when your parents put blinders on you and do their best to bury your dreams. While I'm thankful that my inner spark led me to follow the aspirations in my soul, my heart will forever lament the torment Janine endured. She never really had a chance. She was denied the right to become what she was created to be. We all have our strengths, our inclinations, and the places where our souls find our passion fulfilled. Her parents denied her this. They took a beautiful, loving, and spirited soul, and over time, severed her passions from her. In the end, her choice carried only a faint whisper of defiance toward those who had tormented her.

There are no classes for parents to learn the difference between giving birth to children and ripping apart their souls. As a parent, your job is to love and nurture your child. When you fall short, someone will suffer. It might be the loss of a sweet childhood, or it might be the loss of the sweet child—driven to their demise by you. Neither one is acceptable. Neither is fair. Neither should be an option.

I do know that I took some deep lessons in parenting from losing my friend Janine. When I was applying to college, I knew I wanted to major in art. My mother informed me that was simply not an option. She said that I would starve as an artist and that nursing was what I would major in. I knew that if I wanted an education that they would pay for, it would only involve nursing. Although I do not regret having earned my nursing degree, not a day goes by that my soul doesn't feel short-changed. I was wired to paint. I am self-taught, but I often struggle desperately to create what art training would have provided. That said, when our son Robert decided to pursue Music Industry as his major, I was surprised to hear my inner voice screaming, "YOU WILL STARVE!!" Then, I heard Janine's desperate pleas to her dad—so loudly, they silenced this scream-ing in my own head. I had learned from her death that we were created to make a unique difference. We spend all of our children's childhoods building up their courage to become what they essentially were meant to be and do; how, then, can we swipe it all away, based on our sudden duty to become practical on our children's behalf?

Janine never had the chance to pursue her dreams, but at that moment, her example helped me to remember this important truth. Now, our Robert has an amazing career as a media designer, working all over the world, finding joy in using his talents every day, doing what he was meant to do. May she forever rest in peace, and may her lesson go on to touch those she never could in her life.

November 2003

Happy Autumn, Dear Friends!

I write this on a tranquil Sunday October afternoon, but in my head I envision your mail-person gingerly stepping over and through brilliantly colored, fallen autumn leaves to bring you this early holiday letter. To me, Thanksgiving seems the perfect time to send our love your way. Always, I have felt that there is no better time than the present to go with what your spirit moves you to do. Today, my spirit moves me to sit still and paint a picture of all the things that moved us this past year.

All the days of this past year have simply flown by! We feel like a mother bird, proudly watching our children unfurl their wings, seeking to investigate and understand that which lies beyond their safe little nest. While our nest isn't quite empty, our bank account is... Eighteen-year-old Scott is now a sophomore at Boston College, and he has changed his major to graphic design, with a minor in digital media. As the creator of his own web design company, Scott designs and creates web sites, but he's now also employed by Boston College's Office of Public Relations. Somehow he maintains his perspective, while keeping his heart steadily focused on his girlfriend of two years, Pamela—who is dearly loved by us all.

Robert, currently a junior in high school, continues to audition for commercials and movies in both Boston and New York City, and he had a major role in an independent film. For an English project, Robert chose to make his own rendition of Lord of the Flies. He cast Alexander for the role of Piggy, stuffing his skinny brother with pillows concealed beneath a large jacket. Our dog India was featured as the beast. This tragedy was more of a comedy... Robert is performing in the school play, continues to play drums and keyboard in a band, and is advancing his entrepreneurial career with multiple part-time jobs and eBay wheelings and dealings.

More often than not, thirteen-year-old Alexander can be found in a cozy little spot reading to his heart's content. Recently his class was asked to submit a one-page report inspired by a picture the teacher provided. Alexander's assignment was one day late, but it was eight pages long! Always, his sense of justice prevails; recently he emailed the American Red Cross to share his opinions on their actions. He was in disagreement with the way they handled their international affairs. Ultimately, his cat Timmy owns his heart. Nothing warms my heart more than to see him reading in bed or entranced by the computer screen with Timmy curled in a ball beside him.

Twelve-year-old Jennifer is the one who keeps the ball rolling. Last year she played street hockey, last spring she played roller hockey, and this season she is playing field hockey. This girl loves sports! She's also in love with the most recent of her six past boyfriends… Jennifer is such an unusual blend of so many things; while mostly uncomplicated and no-nonsense, she has an uncommon compassion for all living things. It is heartbreaking to sense her sadness as she attempts to assimilate the loss of two grandparents within the past year. But Jennifer is resilient; her heart will mend…

Ten-year-old Nicole is the epitome of empathy. Often she arrives home from school with stories from her day. One day, in between bites of PB&J, she shared one of the "saddest stories" she had ever heard. She relayed how her favorite friend at school was given a bunny rabbit for Easter. Apparently this friend thought the candy in the basket was food for the bunny. Nicole became very quiet and pensive. I gently asked her how the bunny was now. She replied, "It died! That's what happens when you feed bunnies chocolate! So, if you ever give someone an Easter basket and a living bunny, just put bunny food in the basket. Who needs chocolate, anyway?"

The guy who fulfills all (well, most!) of our wishes is Will. I continue to wonder what we did to deserve this guy! While practicing medicine at three area hospitals, he continues to write chapters and do research. Together, we have attended several medical meetings this past *year, and plan on taking the kids with us to a meeting this February in San Francisco. This sweet guy has a love and devotion for his family that is unrivaled. No matter what he is immersed in, he is never further than a beeper away!*

Immersed in so many things, I sometimes wonder if I really sleep or just exist in a persistent comatose state! Although still involved in a loyal relationship with the washer, dryer, and my Suburban, playing laundress and chauffeur has never really been my aspiration in life. I continue painting murals, and still sew and knit. Recently I made a new acquisition—a new spinning wheel! (My old one was acting like a flat tire.) I must admit that as rewarding as motherhood is for me, it is equally challenging. When faced with the increasing likelihood of impending insanity, I resort to exercise, riding my recumbent bike daily or working out with a trainer. Still, there is nothing I'd rather be than a mother and wife. I couldn't ask for more, and I take nothing for granted—ever.

I have such appreciation for all the blessings I have been granted, including you, whose friendship brings much joy to our lives (while we bring long holiday letters to yours)!

In early March, my father passed away from heart disease on his seventy-fourth birthday. My dad taught me many lessons in life. Three short weeks later we celebrated Alexander's Bar Mitzvah, and I could imagine Daddy's thrill in hearing Alexander flawlessly read Hebrew from the Torah. We were all so proud. Then, in late spring, we mourned the loss of Will's maternal grandmother. There is something so amazing about a woman who dealt with a great many losses in her life, yet proudly held her head high and made friends and admirers no matter where she went. We reminisce about Nana often. In October, we said goodbye to our eleven-year-old dog, Iman. This furry black ball of happiness had been a part of our family since Jennifer was born. She was such a kind dog; her sister India continues to long for her, and so do we.

Although there were losses this past year, we take great solace in knowing that somewhere deep within our souls, we can vacillate between pain and healing, yet eventually we realize that those we have lost will continue to live on within us. The daily comings and goings we shared with them can become beautiful photos we carefully arrange into an album for our hearts.

This brings us to you, dear friends! We wish you so many things for the upcoming holiday season. This past year has taught us to open our hearts fully. Let in all you can, and waste no time—in sharing joy, in letting those around you know how much you love and cherish them, in reaching for others' hearts, and even feeling their pain. As darkness falls, rekindle the flames that warm you to the core. Reach out to spread that warmth, and make it last for the entire winter!

With warmest winter wishes,
Will, Dana, Scott, Robert, Alexander, Jennifer and Nicole Andrews

CHAPTER 10

My Sweet Will

$\mathcal{I}$ hope it's clear by now that Will's presence in my life was an incredible anchor for me, a lifeline holding me up through my desperate attempts at psychological survival. When I met the man who would become my husband, I was only fifteen. I knew I wanted to escape my life as it was, but I didn't know how. My boyfriend before Will had been a young crush, and that experience ended up almost crushing me. That boy constantly reminded me he didn't find me intelligent. He had a mother who was just like mine; she would constantly torment him, and he took it out on me. Looking back, it is sad but not surprising that I would have chosen someone who so closely mirrored my own abusive experience. This makes me feel even luckier that I found Will when I did— before repeating this pattern yet again.

Our synagogue was holding a weekend get-together. It was to be a weekend full of activities, prayer, bonding, and fun, including a chaperoned sleepover. I didn't know anyone who would be there, but I did know that I would make the most of it. Feeling vulnerable but hopeful, I entered the big room, filled with at least seventy-five teenagers. I didn't recognize even one person in this sea of faces. Yet I felt something beckoning me from the left corner of the room. I remember this strange, curious feeling of following a guiding force, and a kind of assured calm that I'd never felt before. It was as if everything around me stopped.

I stood there, facing this sweet, teenaged guy with sensitive green eyes and the kindest smile. We introduced ourselves to one another, and at that beautiful moment, somehow, my heart knew that I had just met my future. We talked nonstop, till it was time to lie down for the night. He shared his pillow with me, and we slept side by side. As young as I was, somehow my soul had met its other half. I was in ninth grade, and he was in twelfth grade. My parents would never let me date an older boy, and he had better things to do than wait for me. Still. I knew there was some soul connection between Will and me.

Soon after, Will went off to college. We exchanged a few letters, and whenever I saw his mother and sister at synagogue services, I'd ask them how he was doing. Two years later, we met once again, at a party for Bianca, who was leaving for college. It felt as if we had never been apart—we just clicked immediately. We caught up on the past few years. He told me about college life at his university, where he was a pre-med student, while I talked about getting ready for my senior year of high school. I mentioned the coffeehouse I was playing in that weekend at a nearby university, hoping he might show up.

As usual, my parents wouldn't give me a ride to the coffeehouse or pick me up after the performance. I had to ask a guy I knew if he would give me a ride home after I finished the show. This guy suggested that we could stop at his house on the way home. I started to get nervous—I was still a virgin, and I knew I didn't want to let him take advantage of me. Then, midway through performing a song I had recently written, I saw my sweet Will stroll into the bar. He had come to see me. He listened intently through the very last song. When I was done, he offered me a ride home. He didn't know at that moment that he was already my knight in shining armor, saving me from an uncomfortable situation—or that ultimately he would save me from so much more.

I was so happy to be with Will. He didn't seem to know what "mean" was. He loved nurturing me. He supported me. He was raised with kindness, unconditional love, a plentiful supply of ice cream, and all the books he could ever want. He held me in the softest spot of his heart, and he only knew how to give me the sweetest kind of love. My only problem with him was that I thought it was all a joke. How could he find me lovable? Why would he waste his time on me?

Both mother and Bianca sensed that Will was different, and they could see the heartening effect he had on me. Of course, that meant that they saw him as a threat to the twisted status quo in our family. They tried to separate us on numerous occasions. They tried telling him I wasn't worthy of him, and that he shouldn't trust me. They warned him that I would hurt him. He politely smiled and walked away from them. Thankfully, from the first, he saw the good in me.

I remember the night that my mother screamed at me, berating me for committing the inexcusable act of revealing her craziness to someone else—the woman I opened up to when I came to babysit her children. Bianca listened as Mother ranted on, accusing me of telling lies about her. My evil sister piped up, suggesting that she and mother would have to tell Will about my betrayal. Once again, they forced me to try to push Will away. Later that same night, when Will came to pick me up for a date, I answered the door. With Bianca and Mother standing behind me, I spoke to him through my tears, reciting the script they had set for me: that I was unworthy of him, and that he should go away and never come back. Will, bless him, sized up the situation immediately. He said we needed to go, took my hand, and we left. He saw through it all. He believed in me. At that moment, I felt safe.

Through the next few years, Will was always there to encourage me, to listen, to remind me of who I could become and all the things I could do and create to touch others' lives. He was there to hold me until the tears dried. He sustained me through those nights when the only way I could see out of my pain was for me to stop breathing in my sleep. He patiently dealt with my anger at my mother, and he didn't laugh when I asked him how many pieces she could be chopped into so there would be none left! He believed in me and had the wisdom to know that I was not a violent person. He valiantly chased away the nightmares, and he was still there holding me come morning. Through every season he has wrapped his arms around me.

Will and I got engaged when I was nineteen and still in college. This was a big moment for me, a promise that I really would be able to make a new life for myself, and with him. I channeled my feelings into this poem.

Hold Me

Hold me long enough
so I'll forget the gnawing pain that torments me from within,
especially at night

Hold me tight enough
so I'll feel that I am just as real as what caused this pain.

Maybe I'll still be here even after you have stopped holding
me—and my pain may not.

Hold me near enough
so I'll listen to your soothing, ticking heartbeat.

It reminds me of the years to come, and the smiles, laughter
and tears (and how they'll REALLY feel!) when this pain is
long gone

Hold me.
Your love has been the only force which held me barely clinging on, yet hoping there must be more. For you I held on—and
you held me.

For me, Will's hugs mean so much more than just a "you mean the world to
me." They remind me that I can finally *feel.* Even after so many years, I revel
in receiving his loving touch and in passing it on to our children. I hug them
each morning, each afternoon when they come home from school, and before
they go to sleep. Hugs are a wonderful way of getting the closest you can be to
another's soul. A wave is just a simple pleasantry, while a hug says, "I truly do
care about you." Never underestimate the power of your hugs. A hug can make
all the difference to someone who is desperately seeking compassion, and feeling so alone. We lose absolutely nothing in giving a hug. For someone barely
clinging to a badly frayed thread, it could mean a world of difference—a world
where they can see themselves living, or a world where they can't.

All of that lay before us when we finally married. I was twenty-one, and
Will was twenty-three. As for the wedding, Mother did her best to make it into
her occasion. She gave me $500 to pay for my wedding gown, veil, and shoes.
She reserved the smallest room at the synagogue for our wedding; then she

explained that, since the room held only 100 people, "You and Will only get ten friends because Daddy and I need to have all our friends there." She went on to try to choose everything else. But I really didn't care; I was marrying the most amazing soul, a man who loved me unconditionally. Who cares about the table flowers and the band, food, and photographer! Still, I did feel the insanity when I was getting dressed in the bride's room along with Bianca and Mother. Trying to find my way into my wedding gown, I called out for help—but they were helping each other and completely ignored my pleas. They wouldn't even help to zip my wedding gown!

I vividly remember standing beside this beautiful, unequivocally loving man at the altar, and telling myself that marrying Will was the only thing in my life that was right in every single way. I knew that he understood me better than I understood myself, and that he was a man of his word. He *would* honor and cherish me until death did us part. I also knew that my heart was, for the first time in my life, complete.

Maybe I can be forgiven if, on that wonderful day, I let myself think that all my nightmares were behind me. I did not want to imagine there would be more heartache to come.

November 2004

Happy Autumn, Friends!

Outside today, it's cold and overcast, but inside, my house is filled with the sweet scent of fall; there are five loaves of pumpkin bread baking in my oven!

Summer is now just a leaf-covered memory. Those lazy beach days, sleeveless shirts, and apricot sunsets have been replaced by the ticking timeclock, turtlenecks, and the treadmill that runs well past nightfall. Still, some things thankfully remain unchanged; our hearts are grateful, our house is noisy, and the front door swings back and forth like a weathervane in a hurricane!

There is no shelter from this storm that is the Andrews household. Substituting the bedlam of our home for the pandemonium of dorm life is 19-year-old Scott, now a pre-junior at Boston College. Scott was crowned Homecoming King last fall, but he currently oversees the peasants on his floor as a resident advisor. He is very active in the regional students' association, while maintaining a web design business with several universities as clients. While my lack of technological prowess poses quite a challenge for me, he is always there to save the day! This summer he bought himself a new Mazda; decorating the passenger seat is his beautiful sweetheart of three years, Pamela.

Robert's plate is always full; at any given time you may find him writing, singing, recording songs, drumming, drawing, or painting. This past year Robert played a lead role in his high school production of Neil Simon's "Rumors." He also acted in several training and education videos. For his English class project he chose to do a "documentary" on Hamlet's sister. He and his crew filmed at a nearby lake. Although it is of a serious nature, picture Robert as Ophelia, clad in a white cotton sundress, with newspaper stuffed in the chest, and swinging his masculine sandal-clad legs while sitting on a tree branch. At the conclusion, poor Ophelia drowns in the lake. Unfortunately, Robert failed to remember that his newspaper stuffing might not remain intact when submerged in the lake. His Ophelia drowns, while the Daily newspaper *floats nearby...*

Alexander, now fourteen, has every weekend planned with the same activity: playing video games, literally from Friday after school until Sunday afternoon, then sleeping until Monday morning. His second love continues to be reading science fiction and fantasy books while cuddling with his cat, Timmy, and our dog, India. Somehow school is just a minor inconvenience. Most of his communication takes the form of Medieval English. The other night when I made him a milkshake, he queried, "Is this some potion of doom?" Alexander and three of his best buddies have embarked upon a new project: writing, acting in, and producing a movie. Through the woods, they battle one another in hooded garb, swords in hand.

Twelve-year-old Jennifer has traded in last year's tomboy clothes for all things pink (excluding her green electric guitar which she plays well, and loudly). Gone is our little tomboy—in her place is stands a beautiful, high-spirited, mature, sensitive young woman. She is very concerned with equal rights for women, and this manifests itself in her playing on mostly male sports teams, and debating both Alexander and Will on any given topic each night at the dinner table. We are in the midst of planning Jennifer's Bat Mitzvah. Recently she and I ventured on a date to the fabric shop, where she selected the material for her Tallit. Together we created a beautiful garment; her chosen quote for the Hebrew on it was, "rejoice in your family."

Nicole's creativity knows no bounds; she appropriates any items necessary to bring her invention to fruition. Now eleven, Nicole is also quite adept at fixing anything broken, including hearts... When there is a crisis nearby, Nicole saves the day bearing tissues and sage advice. Nicole must have been a homeless person in her last life. Always one with a vision, Nicole hauled an empty refrigerator carton into her room and outfitted it with a blanket, pillows, her favorite 24-book series, her current knitting project, a battery-run lantern, emergency flashlight, and Halloween candy. When Nicole steps out of her box, she's cheer-leading for football games, singing in our synagogue choir, and taking weekly voice lessons.

I know there is no Superwoman for me out there, but a wife would be great! Hopefully this wife would do windows and dusting; it looks like Spiderman lives here too. I would welcome anyone who could either take a nap for me or take over for me while I do the napping. My mural business is the cornerstone of my soul. This past summer Robert and I completed a 1,000 square foot mural of Tuscany in the media center of the local high school. I've done everything from tropical teen rooms to fairy tale nurseries, even a gym. Many of my jobs are gratis; I never asked God for this talent and feel that donating my artwork proves my appreciation. On a daily basis I try to laugh heartily and embrace my respect for the fragility of life, thankful for even the menial chores that, in reality, help maintain my humility.

Our very favorite physician is Will, who finds great satisfaction in his professional work. We attended quite a few medical meetings this year, taking all of us to San Francisco and Puerto Rico, as well as New York City and Bethesda, Maryland, for just the two of us. This past summer Will and I celebrated our twenty-second wedding anniversary while visiting my best friend and her family in Florida. How fast twenty-two years have flown by! My husband is kind to the core; he has so much patience, and he encourages all of us to follow our hearts and reach toward all we are meant to be. Due to his devotion and hard work, we want for nothing. For this and, especially, for him, we are forever grateful.

As I write these last lines I find new news to send your way—Nicole has adopted an adorable six-week-old female kitten ("Paisley") from a shelter. Nicole is ecstatic. Even more thrilling is the news that our favorite nanny from California just gave birth to beautiful twin boys. To think that she and her husband met at our front door, and now they are a family of four.

Our thankfulness for you, our loved ones, goes far beyond the miles between us. Wherever you are, find a cozy corner by a window and take in the colors of nature's palette. We embrace your kind friendship throughout all 365 days of the year!

Much love to you and yours,
Will, Dana, Scott, Robert, Alexander, Jennifer, and Nicole Andrews

CHAPTER 11

Can't Get Away From Her

When we first married, we moved into our own little apartment. I loved fixing up our new home. I knew that Will loved me with every single fiber of his being, believed in me without reserve, and lived for my happiness; I, in turn, lived to make him happy. However, my mother continued to live in my head, rent-free, as she continued to take up major real estate of my waking life. Her guilt trips and constant efforts to control us kept me whipsawing from happiness to despondency. Mother would call us at ten o'clock at night wanting to chat and ask what we were doing. Will, exhausted from his long day at work, would whisper to me, "Tell her we are married and have a life!"

Often she would call with the sole purpose of updating me on the latest gossip concerning her friends, none of which concerned or interested me. When Will would gently remind me that this was *our* time to be together, I would sheepishly try to tell her that I needed to go. She would angrily retort, "It's *your* nickel!" Which made no sense, since she was the one who had called us—but that didn't matter to her. I was still so intimidated by my mother, and so desperately fearful of doing anything to anger her, that I would back down and let her ramble on. I'll never forget how these conversations made me feel. I felt inherently bad and selfish for not allowing her to control me. What was wrong with me? Why did I feel like such a "naughty girl"? I felt so torn between my desires—wanting not to give in to her and to have the right to private time with my husband—and my actions, falling into line with her bullying, as I always had. I would patiently hold the receiver and listen to her ongoing ranting about whoever was her latest villain—usually my dad. She would cry to me about how he ignored her or refused to validate her emotional needs. If, God forbid, I stood up to her and told her that he was *my* dad, and she was putting me into an uncomfortable situation, she would angrily retort that I had no idea what it was like to be in her shoes, to be married to a man who doesn't care about you. She would then be sore with me, as well, and, in her usual childish behavior, give me the silent treatment—refusing to talk to me for days and sometimes weeks. That was the only way I gained any respite from her, but it came at a price. During these periods, Mother would also call all of her friends to share with them her report on how disloyal and ungrateful I had been, and to make sure they were still loyal to her. She would also call my sister and brother, and inevitably one or both of them would call me to tell me how much I had upset her.

The worst moment from this period grew out of my mother's twisted, vindictive behavior. We had been invited, along with my parents, to a family wedding in another state. Mother knew we could not afford the cost of plane tickets to attend this occasion, and we weren't particularly interested in attending anyway. She offered to pay for the airline tickets for Will and me. I knew she only wanted us to go so she could show off her married daughter and son-in-law. I was working full time then, as a nurse on a hospital's night shift. She did not work; her personal agenda was what dictated her schedule and everyone else's. She decided that because she was paying for these airline tickets, it was my job to call around and find the best rates. (This was before the Internet arrived.) I pushed back, telling her that most days, I would come home from work exhausted and go right to sleep. This made her irate; once again, I was in trouble.

My mind was telling me to be honest and just say that it was only she who wanted us to go, and that since she had more free time than I did, she could also call the airlines. I knew that her insistence on my taking this on had nothing to do with practicality and everything to do with her need to exert control. In terms of my heart, that was another story. My heart continued to be loyal to her. My heart still believed it would never, ever become whole until she accepted me. The only consistent, clear message I got from her, even after I was married and a mother, was, "We cannot love you unless you change." When it came to a desperate, still unfulfilled craving for my mother's love, I was willing to do anything, including changing.

In that moment, however, my mind overruled my heart. I let her know that I would not be calling airlines, and she was welcome to do this in her ample free time. My challenging her was met with more anger and high drama. First came the tears (Why are you punishing me like this?"), followed by the threats ("Your father and I don't have to pay for you and Will at all."), and finally a long silence. This meant no phone calls to me, but numerous phone calls to anyone who would listen to her woes concerning me—her "selfish, vituperative bitch of a daughter."

I was starting to tell myself that I'd done the right thing, declaring to her that I was no longer playing by her rules—or playing at all. Then one day, while shopping at a neighborhood farmer's market, I was blindsided. I ran into an old friend of Mother's, who looked at me with a sad expression on her face. "I am so sorry to hear about your grandfather," she said. Confused, I asked, "What do you mean?" She replied, "He had a heart attack a few weeks ago, and he passed away several days ago. Didn't you know?" My eyes welled with tears, while my heart plummeted like a stone. I had missed my grandfather's final illness. There would be no last goodbyes, no funeral to allow me to face the reality of his passing. Later, I gathered the confidence to call my mother and ask her why she didn't even have the courtesy to notify me of his heart attack, death, and funeral. Her response made me go cold: "When you refused to call the airlines, I was so mad at you that I didn't care if you lived or died. Why would I then call you to tell you anything?"

I hung up the phone, feeling like I'd been run over. I was angry that my own mother could cut me so deeply simply because of a trivial issue like a phone call to an airline. In taking a small stand against her and honoring myself, I had trapped myself in her web, and I had been desperately wounded yet again. I wondered if I could ever earn a place in her heart without trampling the dictates of my marriage and my heart. My heart wanted out. My soul was tired, dry rotted from years of her use and abuse. I felt lost, with no way out. My own mother apparently had no love for me—or how could she have done such a thing? She had swept me out of her life like so much house dust, and she had informed all her friends and all my relatives that I was out of the picture.

I moved through life, feeling numb. I went to work each night, caring for my spinal cord patients. Their bodies, paralyzed from the neck down, were much like my heart: physically there, but incapable of feeling anything anymore. Each night I drove to work wishing for a drunk driver to hit my car and kill me. Will was deep into his residency, and we only saw each other for two hours a day at best. I tried to find a way to make it appear like I was coping. He knew better—he knew I was dying inside. He felt helpless, and he tried every way he knew to make me happy. His love was the only thing that led me to take one breath after another.

December 2005

Autumn Greetings!

On this stunning Indian summer day, it is hard to deny my senses this colorful quilt of fallen leaves blanketing summer's fading grass. As the squirrels gather food to fill their winter pantries, I am reminded of the accessories of the winter season—heavy sweaters, hearty stews, and happy Andrews who scurry about, emptying our pantry, and shaking the creaky wooden floors of this old farmhouse we call home. I am hopeful that the aroma of my pumpkin-flavored coffee will further inspire me in my attempt to describe the past 365 days. Yes, things are still hopping and kids are still running amok at the Andrews'! Hopefully our annual holiday letter will inspire you to seek a quiet, cozy corner of your "nest" to catch up on the comings and goings of our family.

Mostly, this past September brought "goings." Boston College is now home to two Andrews boys. Scott and Robert are enjoying dorm life in the same building. Scott, now twenty, is a junior in graphic design, minoring in digital media. He spends his downtime as a freelance web designer, and he serves as director of public relations on student government. This guy charms everyone he meets with his sweet smile and compassionate candor. He is also extremely proficient when it comes to his siblings; the girls often go to him for boyfriend advice! I wonder just what we did to deserve Scott; this level-headed, sensitive, and thoughtful guy makes my soul sing...

Singing his heart out is eighteen-year-old Robert, who is a freshman majoring in Music Industry. He has adjusted effortlessly to college life, and he continues to act in commercials, educational videos, and independent films. He plays as drummer, vocalist, and audio mixer for the rock ensemble at Boston College, and one of his paintings won first place in a local art competition. Robert's sense of humor is intact; this past June he cartwheeled his way to collect his diploma at graduation! In his emails, he addresses me as "my fairy princess," addresses his Nana as "babe," and has an uncanny ability to find nicknames for everyone he befriends.

Happiness for fifteen-year-old Alexander consists of endless hours playing World of Warcraft, the most popular MMORPG in the country (for the uninitiated, that stands for massive, multiplayer online role-playing game.) This is a computerized version of Dungeons and Dragons, involving strategy, adventure, and mystery. He continues to climb to higher levels, serving as a major contributor in his guild. Otherwise, he reads voraciously, excels in his high school courses, and is unequivocally adept in his mastery of mockery with his sisters and parents! He attended a cyber camp with some of his friends at a local university this past summer. Alexander has an admirable outlook on life.

Thirteen-year-old Jennifer is the comeback queen—often her retorts land her in hot water! She is never lacking for words; a quick shift of her beautiful dark eyes, and you can imagine where she will direct her next comment. This past summer she practiced surfing at the beach, and in the fall played soccer with her school team, while she continues to enjoy playing electric guitar, skateboarding, and bike riding with friends. Jennifer did a splendid job in her Bat Mitzvah last March. She has taken over for Robert as Alexander's personal groomer—she selects his clothes, styles his hair, and has placed herself in charge of making him look "cool." Ironically, he couldn't care less. He's happy with himself, yet she won't give up!

Nicole, now twelve, freely dispenses her uncommon wisdom; she especially excels in freely offering her often-unsolicited opinions. Last week, as I was putting on my coat to go on a dinner date with Will, she uttered, "You are wearing that outside of this house, in public?" She loves to cook, specializing in eggplant Parmesan and ramen salad. Besides her beautiful green eyes, Nicole's beauty is in her ability to connect with those less blessed than she. At school she has chosen to spend recess with a group of children with developmental differences. There seems to be no limit to her patience and respect for others, no matter what their circumstances. Our precious Nicole will always be the cherished baby of five children, who answers not only to many sibling-bestowed diminutives, but also to the needs of many who cannot help themselves.

My days are spent taking care of household/mother/wife responsibilities, wearing my ever-increasing selection of hats, and opening many doors (washer, dryer, refrigerator, kitchen, and car). I continue to paint murals, and I also make and sell polymer clay beaded necklaces, bracelets, and earrings. I've gotten back to songwriting and guitar (Robert recorded one of my songs and added vocals and keyboard), and found the time to do some sewing. I've been teaching both beading and oil painting, which is so much fun! I look for any opportunity I can find to donate my work in an effort to raise money to help charities. I see so many examples of life's fragility and feel our responsibility to lend a hand.

Reaching into emptied pockets is Will, attempting to pay for two in college and three in braces. This guy is our hero! I find it amazing to realize just how devoted Will is to both his family and his patients. With uncompromised integrity, Will carries on, serving as a marvelous role model for all who know him. Not everyone who knows him gets to see his quick, dry wit. Typically, he refers to the boys as "Chief," but on allowance day, he addresses them as "Thief!" He continues to thrive in his work; when not attending to patients, he enjoys writing and giving lectures.

This past summer we took our dog-and-pony show on the road, to the beach for two weeks. In addition to enjoying Will's parents, we had a lovely visit with his sister and her four children. Will and I celebrated our twenty-third wedding anniversary in June; we've come a long way from that night we met at the ages of fifteen and seventeen. Just last month we said goodbye to our sweet India, who now frolics with her sister Iman in dog heaven. It was heartbreaking to lose her, but at the same time, it was such a relief to no longer find her awaiting her already-departed sister each day by the door. In September we took the kids to Canada for a family gathering. We had an amazing time catching up with relatives and cousins, and we enjoyed a special visit with *my uncle, who's a well-known Canadian artist. It was fascinating to connect with him; he led me to understand and accept so much about my artistic nature.*

How special you are to us, and how grateful we are that God has brought us together. The years pass at lightning speed, but true friendships can weather time and distance. Please keep in touch with us; we're only an email or phone call away! And so… through the next four seasons and the bounty of days in between, we will keep you close in our hearts and at the forefront of our prayers. From the warmth of our hearth to yours, we wish you a holiday season filled with all the simple joys your heart can hold!

Much love from our humble hearts,
Will, Dana, Scott, Robert, Alexander, Jennifer, and Nicole Andrews

CHAPTER 12

One Big Happy

*S*hortly after my mother's vengefulness caused me to miss my grandfather's funeral, I became pregnant. This completely turned me around—Will and I were both thrilled! I had never felt happier in my life. I never doubted I would love motherhood. Everything was working out the way we wanted it; I finally had my chance to fulfill my end of my pact with God. He would give me the children, and I would give them the best childhood, the childhood I had never had. To make things even better, the timing was perfect: it was fall, my favorite season. This time I experienced everything more intensely: the vivid colors of the changing leaves, the orange pumpkins decorating the fringes of the farmers' fields, and the candy apples at the grocery store. When we called my parents and shared our wonderful news with them, they were also thrilled to be having their first grandchild. This happy news was enough to repair my standing in the family.

My beautiful first baby, Scott, was born two weeks late, a big nine-pound, seven-ounce boy. We were over the moon.

Soon, however, my mother began calling incessantly—even more than she had been before. Overwhelmed with dealing with a small baby, we started avoiding her phone calls. Finally Mother left a message, threatening that if I refused to allow her to see the baby, she would take us to court to gain grandparent visitation rights. It was the same old Mother: the world revolved around her, she had no boundaries, and she was insanely punitive. All I wanted was to love and nurture my beautiful new baby and to build a new life with my husband. I would walk to the ends of the earth to nurture my husband and baby, but I couldn't nurture myself. I began to feel depressed and despondent again. How could I love my child when my own mother couldn't even love me?

Will did what he could to help me, but his training still kept him at the hospital for long hours and for days at a time. I started to feel like I was turning into my mother—getting angry at things that should have been insignificant and unable to enjoy the gifts I had in my life. I was living in a world where I had the most amazing husband and child, yet I couldn't feel anything at all. My life looked like a fairy tale, but it was actually Cinderella gone awry. The wicked mother still held the key to my soul.

I tried to keep my little family and myself safe. I avoided going to places where my mother or her friends might be. I refused to answer our phone, worried that it might be her calling. I knew I didn't have the strength to stand up to her. As her phone messages became nastier and more threatening, I felt increasingly desperate. Eventually, I pulled down the shade on every one of our first-floor windows. How sad that I feared I couldn't push her away if she came to my own house! When I was playing with and reading to Scott, life was perfectly wonderful. When the doorbell or phone rang, I crumbled into tiny pieces. Unlike the fairy tales I read to Scott, my story continued to get darker, chapter after chapter.

At night I would lie awake, wondering how I could ensure that my sweet little baby would never fall prey to my mother. It was more than enough that I suffered at her hands, but his innocence and vulnerability to her madness and hurtfulness was more than I could handle. When I finally fell asleep, I endured a recurring nightmare. Night after night, my mother was looming, ready to take everything away from me. Each morning arrived with the hope of a new day; yet another opportunity for me to hope she would finally recognize the dutiful daughter, wonderful wife, and loving mother I was. I cooked amazing meals, knit sweaters, made beaded jewelry, sewed curtains, and even served as a counselor for nursing mothers. I became amazingly adept at busying myself to white out the obsession with being vindicated by my mother's belated appreciation and love.

Will and I decided we felt ready to have another baby when Scott was a year old. I had so much love to give, and I also knew that Will and I wanted to have a large family. Soon we were expecting our second child. Things finally seemed to be on an even keel, but my mother again started calling incessantly. I made the mistake of telling her we were expecting another baby. Her reaction was, "Don't you think that Scott will get lost in the shuffle?" In spite of her verbal sabotage, this pregnancy went wonderfully. When Scott turned 21 months old, we welcomed his baby brother, Robert. The night Robert was born, I called my mother and excitedly exclaimed, "I had the baby! He's beautiful!" She responded coolly, "Who is this?" Her reaction spoke volumes. Here I was, happily embracing the life I had always dreamed of, and she was holding on tight to her old, spiteful tactics. How long did I have to subject myself to her assaults? I knew that I had to be very careful about letting her into my new family.

Slowly, once again, she began to seep into our lives and sap my happiness with her constant incursions. One day I got a phone call from Scott's preschool principal. It seemed my mother felt it was appropriate to stand outside of Scott's classroom, cookies in hand, waiting for the class to take a bathroom break. She would hand him cookies while the teacher watched in disbelief, and the other children looked on with envy. Much to Will's dismay, I could not summon the courage to confront my mother. Instead I asked the principal to confront her and have her removed from the school if need be.

The phone calls continued. My mother would call to reprimand me because it had been several days "since the boys have seen their grandfather." She couldn't stand to be with him most of the time, yet he proved quite convenient when it came to concocting guilt trips for me. According to Mother, the only convenient time for my parents to visit us fell during the boys' daily naptime. I tried to suggest that the two-hour naptime was not the best time for a visit; she insisted that these were the only hours that were convenient for her. Really? She didn't work! Nevertheless, several times each week, my mother and father would come over to our home, march up the stairs to the nursery, and awaken my sleeping babies. Dragging them from their warm, sweet dreams, my parents expected our sons to wake up immediately and play.

Will could not understand how I allowed this. I was keenly aware that the situation was bad for the children. As their mother, it was my place to protect their naptime. But I also knew what I faced if I stood up to my parents. How sad that I was so desperate for my mother's love, and so afraid of her insane overreactions, that I would place her needs and desires before those of my sons. Again I felt twisted out of shape by her machinations, like a piece of Scott's Play-Doh. I was losing touch with my inborn sense that my life was mine to live.

Finally I stopped allowing them to wake up the boys from naptime. To enforce my decision, I also stopped answering the phone when they called, knowing they would just announce their plans to visit. This made Mother furious. So she tried something different: she called Will's parents, and she asked them out for lunch.

At the lunch, she tried to recruit my unsuspecting in-laws to refuse to communicate with me—to show me how it felt to be snubbed. Will's parents had to sit through a diatribe on what a disrespectful, hurtful and ungrateful daughter I was. Of course, my in-laws refused. They told my parents that they respected me, and could not join in this plan. After that, mother passed around rumors that Will's parents were "stupid people." My dear mother-in-law had a hard time with this; her dearest friend had just lost her 22-year-old son, and she could not even begin to understand how my parents could throw me away. I was humiliated by my mother's behavior, yet again. In the end, I had to save myself.

We decided another baby would be a wonderful addition to our family. I became pregnant, but this pregnancy didn't feel the same as my previous two. In a moment of haste, trying to make this pregnancy feel more tangible, I called my mother. *Huge mistake.* I shared with her that I was expecting, but that because it did not feel right, I begged her to please tell no one—not even her friends. She demanded I share my symptoms (of course, so she could share them with her friends) but I refused, telling her I didn't want to discuss it. She got angry, then hung up on me. My father then called and repeated her question. After I repeated what I had said to my mother, he declared, "I am your father and need to be told these things." I reminded him that I had a husband to share these things with.

One week later, I had a miscarriage. Desperately needing and craving a mother's assurance and comfort, I called my mother to tell her what had happened. Her response: "Well, *now* what should I tell my friends?" No concern as to whether I was ok, or needed anything, or if Will needed help with the boys.

My response was, I believe, not only appropriate, but long overdue. I screamed into the phone, "It's a damn shame you never learned to love me like a mother should!"

I hung up the phone, tears flowing and unstoppable. Immediately the phone rang; it was my father, demanding to speak with Will. He started telling Will how much my rude and cold remarks hurt my mother and broke her heart. Will tried to defend me. I felt my dreams and yearning for a healthy relationship with my mother unraveling. My will to try again was gone. Already shaken and depressed after the miscarriage, I now sank so low that I became empty. Without any dreams to cling to, I held onto my sons, mostly to keep them from my mother's grasp. They and Will were all I had left. I would call Will at work, and when he was between patients, he would return my calls. All I could mumble was, "Please, Will, tell me something to make me feel less sad." He knew there were no words to help. He desperately wanted to help me, but he couldn't see how. Mother had no words of consolation or empathy to offer, because that heart of hers was just an empty cave of self-pity that had no room for me.

With Will's support, I contacted a therapist who agreed to see me weekly. After she heard my stories and saw me crying from the deepest parts of my soul, the therapist offered this: "You cannot ever run from your mother. She is addicted to your pain. She will never let you go. You can try, but I wish you luck. She might just take whatever is left of you." I had no more tears left.

November 2006

Fall Greetings, Good Friends!

This chilly, lazy autumn afternoon is everything I could ever want; the crock-pot is filled with my "tailgate" chili, the cornbread is baking in the oven, and the fire is crackling away. Our awesome neighbors next door bring us their annual gift of caramel apples, and the breathtaking Bittersweet growing along our back fence rails bursts with beauty. For us, home is still this old farmhouse with candles in the windows, creaking floors (still generously providing our children's feet with splinters), windows that provide ample drafts to last throughout the winter, and a special warmth that comes from hearts and not just crock-pots, radiators, or chimneys.

Frequently by the fireplace you'll find the warmest of souls, thirteen-year-old Nicole—the "Queen of S'mores." This child finds every season perfect for toasting marshmallows. An eighth grader now, Nicole became a Bat Mitzvah in May and did beautifully in both the Hebrew and chanting. She volunteers in many venues—her favorite involves helping to host about twenty homeless men at our synagogue during Christmas week. Nicole earnestly listens to their stories of misfortune and seems to make these downtrodden souls feel a renewed sense of hope. Besides cheerleading, tumbling, romance, boys, hair, and makeup, she puts her all into singing her heart out. Her voice is pure and magical... except when Will and I are trying to sleep, and she decides it's the perfect time to completely rearrange her room while singing at the top of her lungs!

Time has turned Jennifer, our ninth grader, into an adorable girl with sagacious, stunning eyes, who always has a reassuring smile for a friend in need. At school she often stands up to the bullies to defend those they intimidate. Although small in stature, she can take down someone twice her size—Alexander gave up wrestling with her long ago. She loves playing guitar and songwriting; she and her best friend plan on performing at a coffeehouse in our town. Like Alexander, she reads voraciously. She rarely asks for much, but recently she convinced

Will to buy her a small Bearded Dragon she named Raul Sanchez. Jennifer knows that I am not fond of reptiles, and she takes joy in trying to sneak up on me with Raul...

The question commonly asked (especially at mealtime) is, "Where is Alexander?" The answer is always the same: upstairs in his third floor bedroom, playing World of Warcraft. His cat, Timmy, hangs out with him, watching Alexander battle dark demons. Sixteen-year-old Alexander takes responsibility for whatever is asked of him—including breezing through exams for his advanced placement/honors courses. He is also involved in many clubs this year, including film, robotics, and programming.

Enjoying the sweet life in college is nineteen-year-old Robert. Majoring in music industry and minoring in video production at Boston College, this boy never stops to sleep—he is also campus representative for Apple Computer and heads video production for the Boston College recording company. Robert is continuing his acting career, seen this year in a commercial and numerous educational videos. And he produced and directed two documentaries for Boston College, one of which is being used online. Robert's constant creativity, magnetic personality, unrelenting humor, and boundless energy continue to amaze us.

Living just a block away from Robert is twenty-one-year-old Scott—now president of the student body at Boston College and head of resident assistants in his dorm. Scott continues to design websites for businesses, restaurants, and hospitals through his design company. Like Will, Scott's analytical and insightful understanding of human nature renders him indispensable to everyone around him.

These days, not only do things continue to hop in the Andrews household, but also they bark—in the form of Shadow, the black miniature Schnauzer who has stolen our hearts, along with every single one of Nicole's old stuffed animals. Shadow has unsurpassed love, not only for us, but also for devouring Will's Stephen King hardbacks. Her personality and unmatched ears (especially the floppy one) are irresistible.

Will is the ultimate provider for so many; he provides Boston College with most of his income, math homework assistance to the girls, a lifestyle for which we are eternally grateful, and quick-witted advice that never fails to save the day. Recently, Will was teaching Alexander to drive. Alexander applied the breaks at a red light, and since he saw no cars coming, he began to accelerate to turn "right on red." Will noticed a car coming in the distance and didn't trust Alexander to accelerate fast enough. This normally quiet, calm guy suddenly began to yell, "DON'T, DON'T, DON'T!" It was beyond hilarious! What a gem he is. This man ultimately loves his family more than life itself.

My heart is hopeful for so many things—that my crock-pot will never bite the dust, the dust will never obscure our view, and that this view from my window will be the same next year. I seldom find the time for playing guitar, spinning wool, or sewing, but I make time for my career and passion, painting trompe l'oeil murals. Nightly, as I lie next to the man of my dreams and befriend my pillow, I pray that I'll always remember to embrace each precious day and my desire to create joyful memories for my family. Will and I really enjoy our children. I know that our children will always know we are here to love them…

Twenty-four years of marriage and five kids have shown me that time takes care of itself, and it is up to us to savor each and every moment. I tell our kids that we should be where we are and welcome all that life has to offer. Looking back on the past it is easy to see that there is a plan—not always ours—that causes things to fall into place, just where they belong. We are so small in the scheme of things. Let peace fill your soul despite the noisy confusion of life. Embrace even the unexpected turns; often we make friends and learn lessons when we take these detours. There may be no flags at the destination—just a wiser, sandpapered, more patient and loving soul within us.

In this upcoming season we wish you a Thanksgiving accompanied by all the trimmings: family, friends, contentment, good health, and warmth to keep you cozy throughout the winter!

From our corner to yours, Happy Holidays!
Will, Dana, Scott, Robert, Alexander, Jennifer, and Nicole

CHAPTER 13

On the Edge

Will had been offered a prestigious fellowship position in Washington, D.C. I was thrilled to move away from my mother's tenacious grasp. I began to realize I needed to strengthen my resolve, so that hopefully I might find a better relationship with my mother before we moved to Washington with the boys. I had continued to see the therapist weekly. Despite the therapist's conviction that it would be impossible to separate from my mother, I was still hopeful that I could. The history between my mother and myself consistently proved that there was no way for me to win her love. The truth was, when it came to my mother's wants or needs, no one else's mattered. She could not accept someone close to her having any autonomy; her way was the only way. Yet, I had found the strength to stand up to her in the past, and this gave me a feeling of resolve.

I became pregnant with our third baby just before our move. I loved Will and my boys more than I could ever express—and now a new baby was coming who would also need my protection. I was determined to reclaim myself, my life, and my sweet family, building our lives anew in a new city.

We found an apartment just outside of the city. It was a beautiful two-bedroom apartment on the sixth floor of an elegant old building. I moved with the two boys a month before Will did because he was finishing up another fellowship. I was entering the last trimester of pregnancy and feeling energized. Before we moved to Washington, I sewed curtains and placemats, and I came up with ideas for decorating our apartment. Once we moved, I had the whole place fixed up and looking nice in no time. I took care of getting both boys into school, although they had to go to different schools because of their ages. Each day, I drove both boys to school and stayed busy the rest of the day. I had to prepare for the baby boy we were expecting that February, while making sure things were stable for the boys before little Alexander arrived.

When the boys weren't in school, we had great adventures. We often took the train into the city to go to the museum; even going grocery shopping was fun. The boys loved getting to push their little shopping cart to the market a few blocks away, and I allowed them to fill their cart with goodies: they stocked up on the essentials—whipped cream and candy! We also loved cooking projects. On Fridays we made matzo ball soup and different kinds of challah—raisin, sesame, or egg—for our Shabbat dinner.

We also baked cookies and made fun meals together. Once Will had moved to Washington with us, we saw him a little, but his fellowship was brutal. He was on call from the hospital every other night. When we knew Will would be coming home in time for dinner, we would plan a special theme. One night each of us had to dress up in medieval attire. For that meal, the boys and I made a meatloaf that looked like a castle, with a drawbridge made from zucchini and a mashed-potato moat surrounded by broccoli trees.

Sharing my creative side with them was sheer joy for me. After school we did other artsy projects, like making paintings out of potatoes we carved like stamps and dipped in paint. I really let loose on their birthdays: for Robert's fourth birthday, I made a penguin cake at his request. It turned into a full-out diorama, with Pepperidge Farms goldfish and a plastic deep-sea diver atop the huge blue cake, and little penguins perched on gray frosted icebergs, all carved out of cupcakes. Scott's fifth birthday party had a magic theme: a magician come to the apartment, and we had pizza and cupcakes decorated with magician hats and rabbits. With all this activity, the boys still had plenty of energy, and I'd let them ride their tricycles up and down the long wood parquet floor hallway in our apartment. They also loved swimming in the pool in our apartment building.

I delivered Alexander without anesthesia, by my choice. It was an induced labor, because otherwise, Will might not be able to be there. We got a babysitter for the boys, and I had Alexander after four hours of labor. He was eight pounds, ten ounces, and we swore he looked exactly like Winston Churchill!

We had a Bris for him in our apartment, and Will kindly arranged catering for the occasion; still, somehow I baked a beautiful loaf of challah in the shape of a Star of David, and our lovely neighbors brought a few cakes. It was a very meaningful day.

We made friends in Washington, mostly the neighbors on our floor. It was a year that would include amazing growth and amazing pain. There I was in a new city, with three young children, running constantly with a newborn in tow, and no one to help—or to share the joy with. Will's parents lived within driving distance; they visited a few times, and they developed a wonderful relationship with us and our kids. I knew my mother's aunt and uncle lived in Washington, and I looked forward to reconnecting with them. It was reassuring to me that I would have some family in an unfamiliar city.

Aunt Fiona was one of two aunts who had helped raise my mother—she had lived with them for long periods while her parents were off traveling. In later years I observed that both these aunts (my great-aunts) were mean to their husbands. In fact, they acted a lot like my mother—showing no sense of other people's boundaries and acting rude and arrogant. They also kept up petty feuds between themselves. I would refuse to laugh at their offensive comments, and they resented me for this. Like my mother, they favored Bianca; when Will and I got engaged, they were jealous along with Mother and Bianca. Looking back, it seems likely that these aunts had been role models for Mother; or else, they subjected her to behavior that she then learned and passed on.

One afternoon I was driving to pick up the boys from school, and I saw my two aunts crossing the street right in front of my car. They were so close—but even as I honked and waved, they sheepishly walked away. Something in me collapsed at that moment. Even at a distance of six hundred miles from Mother, I was continuing to pay the price for standing up to her, and I was incurring her wrath. It was clear that she was using them as her puppets to get to me, playing the old game of lining everyone up to shut me out. It was no surprise they treated me this way in Washington, yet I was so vulnerable, so desperate for acceptance and love from my family. I realized that there was no escaping Mother and her little flying monkeys. After that, on many nights after I put the boys to bed, I would sit in the rocking chair as I nursed Alexander, sobbing, sinking into my own bone-deep sadness. How do you give your children every ounce of love you have, when your husband is not home to help you replenish and rejuvenate, and your own mother and all your relatives act as if you are dead?

One of our apartment neighbors died unexpectedly; she was only sixty, and she succumbed to sepsis. Feeling as vulnerable as I did at this time, this news hit me very hard. I decided I wanted and needed to call my father. That night I called him. He spent the entire conversation telling me all about Bianca and her two little girls (despite infertility, she finally conceived) and their new condo—room by room. He never asked about my husband and three boys, and when I tried telling him about them, he switched the subject. Finally, he ended the conversation—politely, but in a very businesslike manner. I hadn't even brought up the sad news I wanted to share with him. I cried myself to sleep that night, and most nights, for much of that year. I wasted so much time pursuing something they simply refused to give me—love and acceptance.

Nor had I given up on the idea of connecting with my Aunt Fiona and Uncle John, even after she had pretended not to see me on the street. After Alexander was born, I invited them to come meet our growing family—they'd never met any of the boys—and have dinner with us. In spite of being flat-out exhausted, I threw myself into the preparations. The day of the dinner, I decided to forego a much-needed nap, and I worked through the afternoon to make an amazing dinner for my aunt and uncle. I was so excited; it was only my subconscious mind that secretly knew I was yet again looking to prove to my mother (by proxy) how wonderful I was.

Eager and anxious, I waited for the call from the lobby to inform me of their arrival. The phone never rang. The clock ticked away, the minutes turned into hours, and they never showed up. Finally I called my aunt. She offered a pathetic and unbelievable excuse: "We were running late and decided it was better not to come than to come late."

I hung up the phone and cried like a baby, my body shaking with desperate sobs. My boys came running to me, and I could barely explain anything through the tears. All I could do was ask them to hold me. This was the first time they had seen what my mother's rejection did to me. They watched as my despair poured out, leaving me deflated and lifeless. The party was over. I tucked the boys into bed, and I rocked my sweet baby Alexander and nursed him to sleep. As I laid him gently into his crib, my familiar pain returned. The therapist had been right. I could never run away from my mother—and I could never find my way into her heart either. I was living in sheer hell. There was no way out.

From this point on, I stopped feeling—it was simply too painful. Will was in the midst of his fellowship and was still on call every other night from the hospital. The nights in between, he wouldn't get home till after dinner, just in time to kiss the boys goodnight. He was completely exhausted, and I was completely numb. I barely functioned. I made sure the boys were safe, fed, clean, and loved—hugging my boys, kissing their scraped knees and elbows, celebrating their lost baby teeth. We continued taking walks, baking bread, and making potato paintings. But once they were at school or asleep, I would just climb into bed and cry. Will held me all the time, and he encouraged me to see just how much he and our boys loved me. All I could see was the stark fact that my own mother could not love me. How then could I love my children, when I was unworthy of her love?

Several months later, my Uncle John called me and told me he was in the hospital, extremely ill. While Alexander napped, I made a pot of chicken soup. That afternoon I took six-month-old Alexander and a huge container of soup and visited my uncle. There he was, looking less than half the man I remembered from the previous time I saw him. He was almost paler than the bed sheets, and he looked like he was barely clinging to life, but somehow he managed a huge smile when he saw me. My aunt Fiona was sitting beside him. Uncle John complained to her that his feet were cold and asked her to put his socks on. Her reply stunned me. "I just took them off! I'm not doing it again," she said. He replied, "But my feet feel so cold." With that, she turned her back and left the room.

I reached for his socks and put them back on his feet. He thanked me with the sweetest smile he could muster. I stayed long enough to feed him some soup and share pictures of Will and the boys, and he loved meeting pudgy and adorable little Alexander. This was his first time seeing any of them, and he and I both knew that this would be our last goodbye. I wanted to cry. I wanted to apologize on behalf of my mean aunt for how horribly she had treated him for so many years. I wanted to tell him I understood that he loved me, and it wasn't his fault that he hadn't come to dinner when I invited them. I wanted to tell him that I knew he had earned his place in heaven. I wanted things to be so different for him. My aunt had put this sweet man through a lifetime of hell. I was determined to make sure he knew his soul was beautiful and his heart was loving. I could not let him die without knowing he deserved so much more.

One week later he passed away, hopefully to a much better, kinder place. We were invited to the funeral, and I knew my parents would be there. But this was about my uncle—not them. I wanted to pay my respects to this sweet man, not have a run-in with them. For Will, this was the first day he would have taken off from work in six months. When I called my aunt to ask for directions to the funeral, she refused to give them to me. Instead, she insisted that we meet at her house and leave from there. Will, knowing my family well by then, cautiously advised me that he suspected this was a trap. I called back and got the address of the funeral parlor, and we went on our own. Years later I found out that Will was right: the entire family had gathered at my aunt's house to confront me. They planned to take turns insulting and tormenting me, until I fell apart in front of them. These people were like a pack of hungry wolves, closing in for the kill. They were after blood, and they were willing to slaughter me in cold blood on the day of my uncle's funeral. For them, any day and any occasion would do.

The funeral was short, my uncle was buried, and they were more than ready to move on. The family planned to sit Shiva at my aunt's house for the week following the funeral. Both Will and I knew I could not go; my family would take the opportunity of my being there to go after me. I baked a chocolate cake and wrote a note explaining that I had no one to watch our boys, and they were too young to come to a Shiva sitting. Will dropped off the cake and the note, and I felt some relief at avoiding a bad situation.

Exactly one week later I received a note from my aunt. She began by thanking me for baking the delicious cake. Her note went on, "I will never understand how you could be so mean and not sit Shiva with us. Just because you hate your mother does not mean you should take it out on me. At least I have a loving niece—your mother. "

These words seared my heart. I could feel myself shriveling with each word I read. Instantly I knew I had reached a new low. This pain had to end.

I took the letter and the boys upstairs to our apartment and put them in their room for naptime. My mind began to reel. I read the letter again, this time on my knees. After reading the final sentence, I curled into a fetal position and wept. I was done. This was a war I could no longer fight. My mother was an assault machine. She had enlisted the rest of her family to seek and destroy me, and they had completed the mission. I had reached the end of a road that led me into a very personal hell. It hurt too much to take another breath. I summoned the energy to stand up, and I headed towards our balcony.

I calmly approached the ledge of our sixth-floor balcony. It was mid-afternoon in mid-September. The world on the street below carried on, the trolley buzzed by in both directions, and I prepared to end my pain by jumping to the concrete below. This was the only way out of my pain. It had to end. The next instant, I thought of my sweet Will. I had no doubt that this man was capable of loving our boys and giving them the character and integrity I would want them to have. Even though I mistakenly believed I was just an encumbrance to him in this life, I felt I needed to let him know how much he meant to me. Even in my immense pain, I needed to hear his voice once more—for the last time. It was only right to make sure he knew that I loved him more than I could ever describe, but that my pain was too much to endure any longer. Years and years of pain, brought on by the very one who was supposed to love me and protect me from pain, had left me crippled and empty. My body had become a useless shell, stuffed only with remnants of what I used to be and could have been. It no longer mattered. I believed at that moment that Will and the boys would truly be better off without me.

I called Will and caught him between seeing patients in the clinic. I thanked him for all the years of loving me and told him *never* to think he didn't try hard enough. As much as he loved me, he couldn't substitute for the love and acceptance I needed from my mother. I asked him to please forgive me. I asked him to promise me that he would explain to the boys when they were old enough to understand, that as much as I wanted to love them throughout their lives and watch them grow to adulthood, I just couldn't stand the pain any longer. I told Will I had complete faith in his ability to raise them to become loving, kind, and gentle beings. At this point I was crying too hard to talk any longer.

As I straddled the concrete ledge, I asked him for one more favor. "Will, please promise me that every single night you will remind them just how much I loved them. I will always be loving them from no matter where I am. And I will love you beyond eternity."

Will calmly asked me to step away from the balcony. He begged me to understand that together we could all find a way to safely walk away from my pain. If I took my life, I was allowing my mother to inflict a lifetime of pain on the family that I had always lived to protect. I was born to love them. If I chose to abandon Will and our sons, I was sentencing them to a life of more pain than my mother had inflicted on me.

It was then that I realized I was already at the very bottom. There was nowhere else to go but up. The thought of inflicting a lifetime of pain on my husband and children sent a jolt through my core. What kind of mother and wife would I be to choose to sentence my family to this misery? How could I wipe way our sons' innocence and childhood in such an irrevocable way?

In this moment, I believe I got another chance, a chance for my soul's spark to shine more brightly. Somehow I had gained a new understanding. I could not make my mother love me, but that was *her* choice. As a mother myself, I owned my choice; and I was bound and determined to love my children. They deserved to know the mother's love I never did. They deserved the birthday parties with a homemade cake, the crazy cheering courtesy of their silly mom in the bleachers at their baseball games, the Bar Mitzvahs, the prom pictures of a handsome tuxedo-clad son in between his mother and father who look like two happy bookends. They were entitled to know what it feels like to have a mother who could turn tears from a scrape into a smile just by applying a band aid with a happy face, who has the power to hug away heartbreaks, and to have someone on the other end of the phone line who will always remind them that they are the center of her universe. This was just too much to throw away.

Will urged me to find a therapist in Washington. By the grace of God, I found Marilyn. This woman, a clinical social worker, was brilliant at delving through the scars to unearth the woman underneath. I will never forget the loving, loyal, and gentle way she reintroduced me to the shattered little Dana, so that I could hug her, love her, and nurture her as my mother had failed to do.

I gently rocked this pitiful child who wanted for something so essential—to be loved. I held her so tightly and sang to her the best lullabies I knew. I looked into her eyes and could see clear into her pitiful soul. She wore her sadness like a thick winter fog. It was a mist that obscured her sight into any kind of future. I told her she never deserved any of the agony and anguish. I told her she was born for great things. I helped her to embrace the pain because this was what would propel her to move beyond it.

With Marilyn alongside me, I safely walked through immense pain. She helped me to assimilate my wounded child with the wounded adult I was. Learning to walk through your pain, then walking past it, is the essence of healing. It is where you want to be, but at times, it seems like light years away. Unfortunately there is no GPS to assist you through a painful journey, especially when you have three kids in tow.

After one of my more emotionally draining sessions with Marilyn, I went home, and this song, "Like a Woman," came pouring out of me. The tune seemed to follow the words almost simultaneously.

Like a Woman

I don't believe I've died,
the blood still courses through my veins.
I won't take this in my stride,
so please, inflict me with pain.
Make me feel again

Like a woman,
so fragile and kind,
beautiful and weak.
Emerging to seek your arms around me,
your plans surround me.
You've been away so long,

it took a song to say.
Go on and pull that string,
just do anything at all.
There's nowhere else to fall.

I fell for you before I knew
I'd spend time alone.
I shiver from the cold,
needing a hold.

So please just be my man
and love me, and understand.
I'll stay forever more
if you remember

What your arms are for,
the words my heart must hear
just keep me near,
otherwise I'd die
so lonely and cold
growing old
needing a hold
fading away
just please stay

November 2007

Autumn Salutations, Dear Friends!

Leaves are falling, the clock keeps on ticking, and once again we send you this seasonal reminder:

a) *Don't worry about the leaves. If writing this letter gets me out of raking them, then reading it could be your excuse, too.*

b) *We send our early holiday wishes... all seven of us, giving you a synopsis of the last 2,555 days.*

c) *Time flies...and so does the money... in every direction except the bank, when Chanukah looms, with eight gifts times seven people!*

d) *You never can tell—you might just get stuck in line on Black Friday, standing behind some overburdened soul... and you will have this year's letter to read and plan your New Year's Eve Dinner menu in the margins!*

e) *Some things never change... same warm and loving wishes, brought to you by the other overburdened soul, sitting here at the same computer with the same view, to update you on the wild and crazy Andrews household.*

The kitchen is once again decorated with grapevine garlands laden with apples, cinnamon sticks, gingerbread cookie cutters, and gingham bows, the oven still yields seasonal loaves and muffins, but the stove has been appropriated by fourteen-year-old Nicole, cooking Eggplant Parmesan (still her favorite) six days out of seven. When not watching the cooking channel while simultaneously concocting a feast, this ninth grader is busy writing and singing her own songs. Gifted with a beautiful voice and an angelic face, Nicole is first in line to comfort those in need of a hug and kind words. When her best friend lost her beloved pet, Nicole baked cookies for her. Nicole's cats, Storie and Paisley, have taken their place in her bed, which substitutes for her office.

Seeking a driver's permit is nearly sixteen-year-old Jennifer; like those signs detailing how many days are left until the holidays, she counts down the time until her permit arrives. Jennifer's favorite pastime is to involve Will in debates. She is relentless, reluctant to ever back down, and refuses to be intimidated. Being the gentleman that Will is, generally as her angst escalates, he shifts gears, allowing his dry wit to take over. At school, Jennifer is often networking with students and teachers to share her ideas and help bring them to fruition—like the school breakfast program she recently worked to initiate. In addition to her schoolwork and activities, Jennifer is working part time at an ice creamery.

Assisting Jennifer in her many pursuits is almost eighteen-year-old Alexander, a senior in high school. He is so helpful in running errands, driving himself and his sisters to high school and Hebrew School, and taking Jennifer to work. Alexander returned to cyber camp for his fourth summer, this time as a CIT. His favorite word, "dirtball," is used to describe anything he deems less than desirable—which would include most of Jennifer and Nicole's friends, vegetables (especially mushrooms), leftovers, shopping for jeans to replace his current ones, and Nicole's singing during his nightly World of Warcraft raids. Not eligible for the dirtball list would be Timmy, Alexander's beloved cat. Timmy will really miss Alexander when college begins...

The coolest cat would be twenty-year-old Robert, now a junior at Boston College. This summer Robert spent a month interning in New York City at Atlantic Records; he lived with a Brazilian DJ and an Italian student in an apartment above a gentlemen's club. Being underage, Robert was utterly helpless when his Chinese food was inadvertently delivered to the club, and he couldn't enter to retrieve it! Robert has been busy producing and editing videos for a number of professional performers, as well as doing freelance work for ESPN and other companies. The creativity that runs through Robert's veins renders him sleepless, yet happy to his core.

Our eldest, twenty-two-year-old Scott, now in his senior year, is taking classes part time while working full time managing department websites, email, and web and print communications. As a freelance web designer, he recently completed work for another university while managing more than a dozen other clients. Living off-campus in a beautiful apartment in the city, he rides his bike to work to stay in shape.

Although Scott, Robert (and soon Alexander) have their digs away from home, our furry little wonders, Shadow and Snowball, get to dig in our own back yard! These two miniature Schnauzers run amok, causing the three cats to hop up onto any surface to avoid them. Shadow, the wise and even-tempered little black sweetheart, is so patient with Snowball, often allowing her to snag her Frisbee, her most prized possession. White-coated Snowball, a hard-partying hooligan, definitely completes our dog-and-pony-show. She's enamored of Will, but loves his den rug even more, biting enough holes to make it look more like crop circles than a carpet.

Despite being pulled in so many directions, Will manages to maintain a clear perspective and steer toward an optimistic outcome. He continues his position at three area hospitals, and thoroughly enjoys sharing his medical knowledge with students, residents and fellows. Will's occupation has taken us to several destinations this past year: we recently returned from Seattle, and he also gave presentations in Victoria, San Diego, and Bethesda. He is generous in so many ways, providing a wonderful lifestyle for our family, teaching good bedside manner to his students, surrendering his worldly possessions to his naughty dog, and handing over hefty checks to Boston College. Will's kindheartedness and devotion pervade our lives.

Since last year, in addition to my mural business, I have returned to nursing. I love my job! After twenty-three years, I am using my BSN; I now get to alternate between my art smock and scrubs (in a vast array of colors). I work part time, transporting medically fragile infants from *their foster homes to visit with their biological families. My heart aches for these sweet little souls, born with the raw need to be loved. Although it can be quite sad to learn of their unfortunate beginnings, it amazes me to see the hope these loving foster parents bring them. When not changing diapers at work, or loads of laundry at home, I enjoy spinning bamboo fiber, knitting sweaters and socks, and gardening (this summer I became the poster child for poison ivy).*

You'll find no complaints here about this past year. In June, Will and I celebrated our twenty-fifth wedding anniversary in Ireland, spending our anniversary night in a castle! While we were staying with Will's parents and his siblings at their beach house, I realized we've been going there since we dated as teenagers; now our kids are that age. This brings so many things into perspective. We can sit and listen to the clock tick, or we can enjoy the moments before they are part of the past.

As always, from all of our hearts to yours, we wish you 365 days full of plentiful play and laughter, memory-making moments, and good health.

With hearts full of love,
Will, Dana, Scott, Robert, Alexander, Jennifer, Nicole,
Shadow, Snowball, Timmy, Paisley, and Storie

CHAPTER 14

Goodbye, Daddy

After Will's yearlong fellowship in Washington was up, we moved to Northern California for his first real medical position. One night, when nursing little Alexander, I suddenly found myself mourning the fact that I never was, nor would I ever be, daddy's girl. I'm not sure what led me to this thought; maybe I had been daydreaming, while holding my little boy, about Will embracing a little baby girl we might someday have.

This was something I had always wanted, yet my mother made sure it would never be. She had warned-off my father from hugging me, on the pretext that it would be "promoting incestuous feelings." Clearly she was threatened by anyone's affection for her husband—even her own daughter's.

A lullaby was playing, the same one I played nightly in our nursing/rocking routine. The sound faded for me as a tune muscled into my head, complete with words, words that would not be hushed or silenced. The words expressed a truth I wish I never needed to know. By acknowledging it, I could begin to imagine a different outcome for any daughters we might have. Every girl deserves to be Daddy's girl, to be cherished, and to live in his heart.

Daddy's Girl
This lullaby still sounds the same.
I'm older now, and so's the pain.
The love's there too,
but you refused.

Daddy's girl will never be.
All I wanted was your love.
Daddy's girl so hopelessly
wanting you to fill my heart.

My babies need me desperately
but I can't seem to find my way
to give them love,
to set them free.

Daddy's girl will never be.
All I wanted was your love.
Daddy's girl so hopelessly
wanting you to fill my heart.

The nights are colder, but the days are fine.
I still surrender to this heart of mine.
My man, he loves me even when I sway.
No, he's not daddy, but that's ok.

Daddy's girl will never be.
All I wanted was your love.
Daddy's girl so hopelessly
wanting you to fill my heart.

The truth is, my father did many things to me that were unforgiveable. He crossed the line, both as a psychiatrist and a father. He could have and should have put a stop to my mother's sickening behavior, at any point in my childhood. He didn't. He allowed himself to be led around by her, and to become her accomplice. He took part over many years in the many put-downs and humiliations I endured, and sometimes even seemed to enjoy them. Over time, my respect for him withered away. He should not

have treated anyone the way he treated me, and he did not deserve to be forgiven.

On the other hand, he was the parent who showed me occasional tenderness and understanding, from the time that I was very small. And his final years with my mother were anything but easy for him. After I had left home for college and then marriage, Mother had found herself in need of another in-house victim. The brunt of her torment, humiliation, and mocking fell on the most convenient bystander—and that happened to be my father. During those years, Daddy came to realize what I had gone through. My mother's ill treatment of him continued into his final illness, when she informed my father that she would not allow him to die in "her house." As his health failed, she went from one nursing facility to another, trying to buy a space for him—but was turned away, because they could not administer the cardiac meds he needed. He complained to me then, "I bought the house. It is my house, too. Where *am* I supposed to die, anyway?"

I also got to hear him say, "Your mother is a son of a bitch. I am sorry for all she put you through for all those years." That was a pivotal moment for me—an apology such as I knew I would never get from my mother. Of course this did not undo the years of pain and torment—they were written upon my heart. The ink was dried. Wishing to undo years of injustice cannot come close to undoing it. But his apology softened my scars.

Finally, swollen and weak, my father was admitted to the hospital, a week before his birthday. On my father's seventy-fourth birthday, I decided to take our three youngest children to visit him at the hospital. We had a lovely visit. Alexander's Bar Mitzvah was going to be celebrated in just a few weeks, and I had embroidered the *tallit*, the traditional prayer shawl, which my father was going to present to Alexander at the synagogue. Alexander donned the *tallit*, and I took pictures of him standing next to Daddy. Dad was lucid, reading the lines of Hebrew I had embroidered. Then, he looked sweetly into my eyes, and with utter conviction and a sense of elation, said several times, "things happen *so* fast!"

Then he breathed his last. I hugged him and said goodbye.

Where was my mother that day? Not visiting her husband in the hospital on his birthday; she had gone out to play Bridge with friends. She only found out what had happened when she called home to pick up her messages, and she heard me telling her that Daddy had died. As I learned later from one of her friends, she then stood up to leave and said, "No one is to know where I was or what we were doing."

Looking back after all these years, it was a great gift for me to be able to say goodbye to him and to be there with him in that quiet moment. It felt as if the universe was unfolding as my father journeyed painlessly to where he would be forever free and joyful. My dad taught me many lessons in life; it was time to let him go, but I hope never to forget his last, prophetic words. Three weeks later we celebrated Alexander's Bar Mitzvah, and I could imagine Daddy's thrill, and his pride along with ours, in hearing Alexander flawlessly read Hebrew from the Torah.

In this eulogy I wrote for my father, I returned to the experience of being with him at the end.

EULOGY FOR MY DAD

Dad, we honor you today. We honor all the things you were to so many. More than all the things you taught us, it was really the things you showed us that formed us. You made each of your three children feel, on any level, at any given time—that it was ok to feel comfortable in our own skin.

Your humble beginnings have been the common thread that wove your generation to your children's generation. Were it not for your father, as a young man who was armed with expert tailoring skills and a fierce, determined will, I, my two siblings, and your ten grandchildren would not be here for you today.

Daddy, we remember such a multitude of events we shared that we will be forever grateful for! The graduations, weddings, births of our children—these filled you with the immense joy that you held dearly when you breathed your last.

Tuesday was your birthday. Being a fair distance away, my family and I planned on joining you this Saturday to celebrate. That morning, however, a compelling force begged me—implored me—to gather our three youngest children from school. Yes, Daddy, I yanked them out of lunch because somehow I knew that this day was so much more important than any school meal could ever be! Strangely, and quite serendipitously, on my way out the door I grabbed two things: my camera and the tallit I sewed for Alexander's upcoming Bar Mitzvah.

From there, the sequence of events that unfolded could not have been better planned. After we secured your birthday balloons, blooming spring plants, and your favorite dessert—Halvah—we brought our party into your little hospital room. Your eyes lit up as you pointed to Alexander, Jennifer, and Nicole! They climbed upon your bed to nestle close to you. I took pictures of you with them, and one very special one—of you with Alexander, wearing his tallit, that you had placed around his shoulders. You read the Hebrew ("Justice, justice shall you pursue") and we talked about how you were to honor your ancestors through this tallit presentation.

After that you sweetly looked into my eyes and told me this: "Things happen so fast." At first I didn't realize the profound meaning. Then you repeated it twice more—and this time my heart heard these words, which I want all of your hearts to feel, too.

"Things happen so fast" meant so many things that very moment! It meant that in an instant little James [Lawrence's son] screamed his way into the world three months ago—this beautiful infant who would carry on for you the family name! It meant that in life so many things, both happy and sad, can happen—so fast!

It meant that like that morning, we should let God guide our hearts and move us to where we need to be. It meant, waste no time, don't fret about the small things—but most importantly—don't hold anger, hatred, or resentment in your heart. These things take up space where, instead, love can grow! How ironic, Daddy—although in the end it was your heart that failed—it was your heart that spoke words louder than any voice ever could.

And lastly, Daddy, and God, I thank you both for allowing us to share these last special moments together. I felt that although we had times when we were not in communication, we were always connected in our hearts. God, when I questioned whether you were really there, you led Daddy to my door to ask that we resume our relationship. Alexander, Jennifer, and Nicole knew Daddy the least of all of his grandchildren. How wonderful that you chose the four of us to be with him in the end.

Always, we thank You, God, for all the gifts You offer us. But this one was so much more, so much better than any of us could ever have asked of You or Daddy. Our dear, sweet Daddy, the universe unfolded as you humbly and painlessly journeyed to where you will forever give grace to us all. For us the stars will shine brighter and the nights will be more serene because with your beauteous spirit, heaven is now a more amazing place.

November 2008

It's a crisp and sunny Saturday morning here. I've cozied myself into my favorite kitchen corner to view this awesome autumn day. There are pumpkins decorating the front porch, apples baking in my oven, and a lush blanket of leaves on our lawn. Trust me, there will be no leaf raking on my part; I only do holiday letters!

Like last year, same season, same writing desk, same view... new holiday letter, new computer, new lessons learned. Another chance to rekindle old friendships, reach out to new friends, and touch souls forever cherished. Since last year's letter, many things have remained the same, yet many things have also changed. We still live in this old colonial farmhouse complete with drafty windows and squeaking floors. My hundreds of houseplants continue to thrive, the many picture frames still hug our favorite photos, and the leather family room furniture is still as comfy as ever. Perhaps that is because there's more room on the couch these days...

Now all three of our boys are living in Boston with their own couches to jump on—I mean, sit on. Twenty-three-year-old Scott will graduate this spring with a B.S. in graphic design and digital media. He has been working full time at Boston College in the Provost's Office as a graphic designer and web developer, while completing his degree. Scott's integrity is unwavering. When Will and I were away for the weekend recently, Nicole's life fell apart (i.e., she found out her boyfriend will be headed to college in Scotland.) She called Scott to inform him of the devastating news. Within one hour, flowers in hand, Scott and his sweetheart Pamela appeared at Nicole's bedroom door. While Pamela provided the loving hugs, Scott explained (in Scottish dialect) how absence makes the heart grow fonder. Then, this generous guy took his girlfriend and sister out for ice cream sundaes. He will always hold the key to his baby sister's heart.

After two years of babysitting freshmen as a resident assistant, twenty-one-year-old Robert has moved into, renovated, and painted an off-campus house, where he lives with three college friends. This past summer he lived near New York City, working for Atlantic Records full time, creating videos for music industry giants like Kid Rock and Jason Mraz. While working there he rented a couch in a good friend's apartment near Manhattan. Occasionally when he stayed late at work, he would sneak into his boss's office and help himself to a real couch... On the last day of work, Robert misplaced the key to the computer lock somewhere in Manhattan; somehow he talked a locksmith into lending him a four-foot bolt cutter for an hour. There was Robert, running like the wind for ten New York City blocks with a bolt cutter more than half his size, hoisted on his shoulder like a lumberjack.

Speaking of keys... Eighteen-year-old Alexander, now an engineering major at Boston College, left his room late one night, only to find that one of his roommates was drunk—I mean, sleeping—and had inadvertently locked Alexander out of their room. Sheepishly, Alexander had to take the elevator down to the lobby in his boxers to obtain a spare key. Tall and lanky, he swings by on some weekends to snuggle on the couch with the dogs, who he refers to as his "ladies." Alexander has an admirable outlook on life; World of Warcraft raids, cookie dough ice cream, and whipped cream are the essential elements for pure happiness.

Sixteen-year-old Jennifer marches to her own beat, on a relentless mission for her latest "cause of the week." In one five-day period, Jennifer raised over $200 in donations to support awareness of and intolerance to harassment and bullying. A junior in high school, Jennifer has her eye on a career in criminal justice, while her hands grip the handlebars on her shiny, red moped. When Jennifer's chauffeur (Alexander) left for Boston College, she decided she needed a dependable ride to her jobs. She located a moped, earned money to buy it, and got her moped license. Last March, Jennifer spent ten incredible days touring Israel with her confirmation class. I will forever cherish our Starbucks dates, her little "sick visits" when I am the substitute nurse in her school, and her no-nonsense approach to the way things are (and should be, according to her!)

On any given afternoon you can find fifteen-year-old Nicole, a sophomore in high school, in her favorite spot—on the couch, snuggling with the dogs. As long as I agree to clean her pans (not one of her interests), she will offer to make dinner. Not needing a recipe, this girl whips up anything from three-cheese macaroni casserole to lemon squares. Sure as the moon will rise, each night at ten o'clock, you will hear Nicole singing at the top of her lungs. This past summer she played a role in High School Musical, and she did an incredible job. When she returns from school (or the mall), she will find me and ask to snuggle. I am so very grateful to be the recipient of her warmth and compassion. Nicole's dreams include a career in nursing or medicine, which would provide the perfect place for one whose heart knows no bounds.

This holiday letter-writing momma is wearing so many different hats that by the end of the day I do drop to the floor! I'm working with two nursing agencies making new mom/newborn visits, giving injections, and teaching various aspects of wellness. I also substitute teach, and I'm a substitute nurse for the schools in our district. While in the process of becoming certified as a forensic nurse, I have been hired to work with three hospitals as a sexual assault nurse examiner. And I continue to paint murals. The only guarantee in my life is my "rule of opposites": whatever was supposed to happen will not, and what was not supposed to happen, will! Plan B then kicks in, and I follow my most important credo—if it isn't fatal, it doesn't matter!

Will keeps wondering how one envelope sent to Boston College drains his entire bank account. He does, however, consider himself wealthy when it comes to blessings. He is generous in so many ways, teaching wonderful bedside manner to his students, providing a wonderful education for our family, and giving dog bones and Frisbees to the real thieves in this household—Shadow and Snowball. Will's occupation has taken us to several destinations this past year, including Chicago (I hugged Oprah in her lobby at The Ritz!), and on a family trip to California, where we visited our former nanny and her family. This summer we had a wonderful time at the beach bonding with Will's parents and siblings. We continue to savor all the lasting memories that we made.

I keep wondering where the years have all gone. The little ones who used to threaten to run away, now come back home just because they miss us (or they're hungry). The kids who used to fight over computer time now build their own computers. The little girls who sold Girl Scout cookies now bake cookies from scratch. Those little love notes I used to put in the lunch boxes? Now little notes are written by our kids at college and delivered to me along with flowers. This adorable husband who held my hand when we said "I do," held his ears through my five childbirths, and still holds the key to my heart (though he sometimes calls me Imelda Marcos for my growing shoe collection)—he just bought an Adirondack love seat for us share.

And so, another holiday season is here, bringing us another chance to spread the warmth from our hearts to yours. Wishing you 365 chances to achieve all the blessings you desire!

With love,
Will, Dana, Scott, Robert, Alexander, Jennifer, Nicole, Shadow, and Snowball

CHAPTER 15

This Little Star

"**Y**ou will make a magnificent human being."

I sat there in shock. I had never heard such words from anyone—although Will constantly let me know that he loved me and believed in me. By this time, we had been married for eleven years; our family had grown to include five children: Jennifer and Nicole, the youngest, were then four and three years old. Yet my old demons had caught up to me again; for months I had languished in severe depression, unable to see myself or my life as anything but a hopeless failure.

The woman who said this to me was a therapist in an outpatient psychiatric treatment program I had entered, near where we lived. We were sitting in a group therapy session, and I had just offered some words of hope to another patient in the group. I was overcome by a flood of feeling. How could anyone else see my future in such positive terms? How could I? My childhood and early adulthood had been devoid of love and nurturing from my mother—the kind of nurturing that helps a child grow into a confident adult. And there had been hardly anyone else I could turn to. All my grandparents, aunts, and uncles lived far away. My father was involved in his work and avoided Mother as much as possible. Because of my isolation, my only exposure to normal households was when I played with the neighborhood children or a friend's parent would pick me up. When the friends went home I was sent back to my room. With the exception of my friend Christine's mother, I had no alternative to Mother's destructive behavior. Living with constant rejection and the uncertainty of ceaseless game playing—with me as the game piece—I could never find a true sense of self or safety. Mother violated my trust so frequently that

I felt everyone, including all our relatives whom she called long distance to share her woes about me, hated me and knew I was "a loser." By this time, I had become an adult with a truly terrible sense of myself, who would be shocked that someone might see me as good, let alone potentially "magnificent."

I had always sensed that my mother had been terribly damaged by her own childhood experiences. Something had to have caused her frustration, anger, and emotional instability. She wanted to be a valued person and a caring mother—I wanted to believe that—but she was stuck inside this flawed existence that she never chose to repair. She walked through her life with her demons on a leash, allowing them free rein towards anyone who made her feel invalidated or insecure. There was no limit to the degree of retribution she would pursue, as long as she felt it restored her power.

This was the mother who had shaped me. And it wasn't the first time I had been flattened by depression. Even before I left home, when the verbal abuse, public embarrassment, and punishments became overwhelming, I would become despondent and depressed. Sometimes I would think of ways to kill myself. Always, I would revert to wondering if maybe I was incredibly flawed and there really was no place for me in the world. Maybe, no changing in the world would make me worthy of being loved. When people expressed feelings toward me, I could never tell what was real. The only thing I did know was that if I survived that household, I would someday hope for the chance to do the exact opposite for my children. But then I would hear those terrible words reverberating in my head, so often spoken by my mother: "I hope you have three girls *just like you*. That is what you deserve."

The trigger for my latest paralyzing depression had again been my mother—combined with my lingering desire to gain her love and approval. Wanting her to see how well we were doing, I wrote to invite them to come visit. Mother wrote me back saying that they couldn't—because she had a dentist appointment! Her dentist happened to be Bianca's husband, which made the rejection sting that much more. This was such an incredibly lame lie, and it left me devastated. I fell into a deep depression after that. It was hard just to breathe, and I wanted to die. I gained a lot of weight because eating was the only thing that appeased my despair. Will was so concerned about me, he persuaded me to enter the partial-hospitalization program.

During my week in this treatment program, something in me had begun to open up. I had been in individual therapy for a long time, always finding a new therapist to work with whenever we moved to a new city. In this program, I began to see how others, too, had parents like mine, who had crunched their souls like empty soda cans. I also began to experience the beautiful way that the staff brought out our humanness and belonging.

When that staff member smiled sweetly at me and shared her positive vision for my future self, something opened up inside me. I saw myself as a star whose light had been dimmed, unable to shine as brightly as it could among the countless stars in the sky. I excused myself, asked for a piece of paper and a pencil, and began to write. What poured out of me in less than five minutes was this poem.

This little star
This precious little soul of mine
    had sights set on the stars;
you crushed and so belittled it
    then placed it behind bars.

"If only I could jump a little higher"
    I would say.
But higher wasn't high enough
    and you pushed me away.

The days would come, the days would go;
    the soul would flicker still.
You fed upon a steady flow
    you never seemed to fill.

Ironic, though, the soul broke free
    but you remained a child.
Still failing to fulfill a need:
    begging all the while.

The wounded soul would try to heal
    the scars that brought red tears,
but gold and diamonds cannot seal
    what's tucked behind my ears.

Obsessed with feelings of unworth,
    the soul began to die.
The very one who gave it birth
    still crushed it like a fly.

A simple need the soul possessed;
    to love that wounded child—
and finally put their pain to rest
    so they could reconcile.

The child still sleeps, the nightmare keeps;
    the soul has flown away.
But deep inside her heart she weeps
    and tries to face each day.

This lonely little soul soon found
    a new moon by her side.
Together they were tightly bound,
    a universe of five.

How could this little languored soul
    protect these little stars?
Perhaps she'd keep them in the hole
    that used to be her heart.

And as the years spun evenly
    she watched them brightly shine.
From pain turned strength and love
    she never thought she'd find.

> And if inside, you share the pain
> this little star endured,
> this poem won't have been in vain
> and you will know your worth...

This woman's words had scraped up against my greatest fear: that I'd been so damaged by my own childhood that I would be doomed to visit that pain on my own children. The "little star" that was the spark of my true self was now the mother of five "little stars." My fear of failing them, or somehow even harming them—in spite of my overwhelming love for each precious child—had paralyzed me. How do you give your children something you have only heard about and wished for? How do you overcome the numbness caused by your soul being bound and suffocated, to show your own child their worth? I had watched parents interacting with their babies; I could feel the joy and love they have for this gift of life they have been entrusted with. I clearly remember from early on in all of my pregnancies, feeling that extraordinary desire to protect my child from anything and everything throughout their entire lives.

From the moment each of our babies screamed their way into our lives, I remember feeling both joy and fear. I was overjoyed to finally meet, face-to-face, this little one I loved from the very start. More than anything in the world, I felt unequivocally fortunate to have a healthy baby, and I couldn't wait to take this tiny being home. I would do everything in my power to give them the childhood I never had. They deserved nothing less. This, I knew without a doubt.

Our two girls were very close in age: I had gotten pregnant with Nicole when Jennifer was only six months old. Will was worried about the expense of raising a fifth child. I had reminded him how I, too, was an unplanned baby, and this offered a perfect chance to undo the legacy passed from my mother to me: holding a child responsible for "being a mistake." This was truly a gift from God. I knew I couldn't live with myself if I ended the pregnancy. But there was another issue that also worried Will: I had just been given the MMR vaccine, on the advice of my doctor. Both Will and the doctor who gave me the vaccine suggested I terminate the pregnancy. I did lots of research, and I found nothing to suggest that the vaccine crosses the placenta or causes any issues. Thankfully, our fifth child, Nicole, was born blessedly healthy—although with two little ones, we hired a nanny to help out. Experiencing my pregnancy with her had made me, if anything, even more aware of the preciousness and vulnerability of each new life.

The fear I felt, beyond the sense that it would be impossible to shield each child from every hurt, was that my own psychic scars might keep me from fulfilling my pact with God: to raise children who felt safe and completely loved. The aching memory of being made to feel inherently flawed, unintelligent, inconvenient, and unloved formed a cloud that lingered over me, leaving me vulnerable to fear and self-destructive behavior. In spite of Will's sweet constancy and my children's unquestioning love, I doubted my worthiness to be loved and to successfully love them.

Looking back on that moment, I know now that my greatest fear was of harming my two girls—the youngest of our five children. Irrational, yes; but they were the children who were most like me. For me, as a mother, to in any way hurt a little girl—this was too searingly close to my own history. In the poem, I referred to "a universe of five," but in my heart, I knew I was most frightened of repeating history with my Jennifer and Nicole, my two little girls.

That poem recorded a breakthrough for me, allowing me to imagine a life where I could acknowledge the reality of my own terribly scarring past, and at the same time find enough love within myself to share abundantly with my family.

I think my depression was rooted in my deep desire to finally be either accepted by Mother or be healed—so I wouldn't ever repeat this abuse toward them! As painful as it was, I knew that I had to eradicate the demons that threatened to turn me into my mother. I could never allow that to happen. Will was so supportive; not only did he want to help me deal with these devastating demons, but he was more than willing to shoulder the cost of my treatment to help me heal. He understood it as an investment in our children's future.

While I was in the treatment program, a psychiatrist said to me, "You do know your mother is Borderline, don't you?" I had heard this diagnosis mentioned when I was in therapy before, but I hadn't really understood. I asked him, "That means borderline crazy, right?" He rolled his eyes. Then he gave me the full diagnostic term, Borderline Personality Disorder, and said it is a nightmare for patients, their families, and the therapists who attempt to treat them. He described for me the symptoms and behaviors associated with this diagnosis. People with BPD are known for attempting to dominate and control those around them; for constant verbal assaults; for subjecting loved ones to emotional blackmail and manipulation; for compulsion to violate boundaries; for cycling between need and rage; and for the constant state of conflict or crisis that they stir up around themselves.

He had described my mother's behavior in every detail. In a way it was a relief for me to know that her craziness had a name. On the other hand, I'm not sure that it eased the painful effects of having been brought up by her. I urge anyone who has endured any kind of abuse, not just the kind I experienced, to know that its aftereffects do not go away. Abuse, whether endured for a shorter or longer period of time, leaves a trail of debris, shrapnel that becomes embedded in our souls and cannot be removed. The life of an abuse survivor is like a minefield with buried explosives, threatening to detonate even in a seemingly benign moment. Those who have endured this mistreatment have no ability to reason through their pain. We are far too busy juggling a multitude of destructive, negative feelings we direct inward, to finish the job of the perpetrator.

We can only hope that our own innocent children will not become collateral damage, or far worse, intended victims. Abusers cannot comprehend the effects of their actions upon their victims, especially when their own mistreatment is all they have ever known. Abuse, like history, often repeats itself. Let's put it this way: imagine how terrible it would be if your identity were assumed by someone else. Everything you thought you owned suddenly seems imperiled. They can spend your money, use your name, and your life is at their mercy. An innocent child has so much more to lose. Trust, innocence, and the expectation of loyalty from those who are supposed to protect them—are snatched away and smashed mercilessly, to the point where they can't be repaired.

When I was a Brownie leader, I gathered all of our girls, and we did an exercise to try to convey to them this truth of the power of such destructive behavior. Together we traced the outline of one of the girls using crayons. We colored in her clothes and gave her a pretty, smiling face. Using scissors, we cut out this image, and we sat in a circle on the floor. I explained to the girls that we were going to pass the paper girl around the circle. Each Brownie was to say something unkind to her, then crumble a part of her before passing it on to her neighbor. They said things like, "You are not my favorite friend," or, "Your clothes are not pretty." Eventually, after all the girls passed her around the circle, we ended up with a crumbled ball of paper, which resembled nothing like what we started with. Then, we passed her around a second time. The rules changed; each girl was to apologize for what she said and attempt to restore this paper girl her to her original state. Needless to say, this was not possible. It was a harsh lesson, but it was so important to me to impress the message into their hearts.

You cannot take back words, actions, or the painful aftermath resulting from them and expect the victim to remain unscathed or unchanged. You also cannot wipe away your own painful past; but you *can* reclaim your personhood. There are so many avenues of support available. I never asked for the childhood I was given, but I *did* ask for help to overcome it. For that, my family and I could not be more thankful.

November 2009

Autumn greetings to you and yours!

Like a feisty old friend, fall has come to visit once again, bringing vivid leaves that ribbon through the cool, crisp air towards the fading grass below, the farm-stand pumpkin pie and apple cider, and the annual pilgrimage of all my favorite hand-knit sweaters to the front of my closet. My list of things this fall has not brought would include: a team of five leaf-raking elves, a type of Halloween chocolate our dogs won't ingest to the point of near-death, a Starbucks that delivers, and someone to write this annual holiday letter for me...

This three-ring circus that is our life now includes a petting zoo as well! With great gratitude I repeat my yearly slogan, "Things are always hopping in the Andrews household." Additionally, they bark, meow, and eat crickets! One who doesn't read the newspaper, Raula, Jennifer's Bearded Dragon, enjoys living over newspaper, while ingesting a diet rich in crickets. (Jennifer has decided that Raula is a she, not a he.) This twelve-inch reptile happily watches life through the walls of her glass home.

Seventeen-year-old Jennifer, on the other hand, watches the world through the windows of the Dodge Durango she recently purchased. These days, she spends much of her free time working as a server at a local restaurant. We just love to go there as a family. There she is, trying her best to pretend she doesn't know us, but then her manager comes over and tells her that her family's dessert is on him! She has been accepted to the University of Vermont, hoping to pursue a career in criminal justice, and she awaits word on several other colleges. Jennifer is very passionate about equal rights and is very outspoken when it comes to her opinions.

At any given time, you can find 16-year-old Nicole either in her room, singing to her heart's content, or in the kitchen, whipping up her latest creation in a mad mess. Finding inspiration from numerous cooking shows, Nicole creates various tasty concoctions, while rarely relying on recipes. When asked what she wanted to be when she grows up, her response was telling: "I just want to be someone people can look up to." This describes beautifully Nicole's daily mission—to make a difference for others. Currently she volunteers answering phones for a program offering inebriated students a safe ride home with concerned and loving volunteer parents, and she also volunteers at an abuse prevention program.

Back in school is twenty-four-year-old Scott, who, after completing his undergrad degree last June, is enrolled in the information systems master's program at Boston College. This gregarious guy got hired during his senior year by the office of the provost, as their graphic designer and web developer. The design firm he started with five other Boston College grads, specializing in web and print design, is busy with a number of clients. Scott still lives in the city with his stunning and sweet girlfriend, Pamela.

Unpacking the last of his boxes in his New York City apartment is twenty-two-year-old Robert. Robert shares his fifth floor abode with two of his best buddies. After graduating from Boston College in May, he moved to New York, where he is freelancing as a media designer, video producer, and editor on a number of exciting projects. Several weeks ago, I received a call from Robert's cell phone number, but I didn't recognize the female voice. Robert doesn't know her name—only that she lives on the streets of the city, she was very hungry, and his date for that night stood him up. When he passed by this homeless soul and read her sign, he asked, "Would you like to be my date at McDonald's tonight?" She asked him to call his mother, reached for his phone, and thanked me for raising such a kind child.

Nineteen-year-old Alexander is now a sophomore at—you guessed it—Boston College, majoring in engineering. Alexander is attending school full time while working part time as a teaching assistant in the computer science department. Last summer Alexander worked full time doing community organizing. For nine forty-hour weeks, he drove across

Massachusetts assisting with voter outreach events. If you ask him about his future plans, Alexander will tell you he aspires to be "an architect for people's dreams, one who engineers the solution to people's problems, and an inventor extraordinaire." If only he were more ambitious...

The one surrendering his entire paycheck, life savings, retirement, and spare change wallet to one Boston College would be Will. It is completely heartening to sense this man's deep devotion to his profession and the patients he treats, but there are no words to describe the unequivocal love he has for his family! While Will's ability to see all things from a fair, humorous, and loving perspective is to be valued, his overwhelming unselfishness, humility, and integrity render him such a wonderful role model for us all.

That leaves the mom/wife/holiday letter writer/prankster of the family. I continue to wear myriad hats, but can never have enough shoes... I am working as a substitute school nurse in two districts, and as a visiting nurse specializing in Crohn's disease injections. I earned my forensic license, and along with an amazing team, I serve as a sexual assault nurse examiner for three hospitals under the jurisdiction of the prosecutor's office.

This past year Will's work took us to Las Vegas, Chicago, San Francisco, and Bethesda, Maryland, and we spent ten glorious days with the kids at the beach. With three of our children living on their own, we cherish every moment we have together as a family. We are so humbled by the integrity and respect we see in our children; we take neither them nor their qualities for granted.

Looking back over our last fifteen years' worth of holiday letters, I realize how quickly life unfolds, how fortunate and blessed we are, and how many friends we have made and kept as we moved cross-country twice! Even those friends who have passed on live on in our hearts by the many things they did to touch our souls. Really, this is the most important lesson time has to teach. The tide washes in and out, and the seasons come and go, but it is indeed up to us to capture the moments to touch others' souls!

As the temperatures tumble, the white winter skies will surrender their treasure trove of tranquil lace snowflakes. We will welcome the warmth from the hearth as our hearts reach out to yours, wishing you a holiday filled with all you desire and the best of health to enjoy it all throughout the year to come!

With all our love,
Will, Dana, Scott, Robert, Alexander, Jennifer, and Nicole Andrews

CHAPTER 16

I Survived

When I think about our time in each of the cities we called home, I remember so much. Our family had such great adventures. Will moved forward with his work, we made many wonderful friends, and I took on new and fulfilling activities. The excruciating pain I continued to feel in relation to my parents and sister was also undeniably part of that time, but there were also many magical moments of joy and sheer fun with my sweet family. Our first holiday letter was written while we were still living in Northern California. I hope I can be forgiven for leaving out those terribly difficult parts—it was a holiday letter, after all. And it would be many years before I had the strength to start telling the other side of my story.

I did write some more songs and poetry during that time—I could never give up those expressions of my deepest self. Even though I didn't have much time to paint, I did a lot of illustrating, and I painted a few murals. Mainly, I found creative projects that could include the kids. When Robert needed to make a castle for school, we baked bricks of different colors out of cookies and built an edible castle covered with vines of green frosting. For Halloween, we made a mermaid scarecrow for the yard, and I made Halloween costumes for all the kids. One year I made "Three Little Pigs" costumes for Alexander and the girls—Nicole always loved pigs—and our nanny dressed up as the big bad wolf. The older two boys were transformed into a life-sized cow.

It was there that I fulfilled a long-held dream—learning to spin my own wool. I had seen a movie in my third-grade class about Colonial Williamsburg, featuring a woman spinning wool. I knew immediately that I had to learn to do this. This desire had never left me, but it would be a long time before I could act on it. When I spotted an old spinning wheel in an antique store, hanging from the ceiling, I knew it was coming home with me. We bought it, and I searched till I found a woman who lived on a nearby farm to teach me how to spin. In three lessons I learned the basics of spinning wool: how to wash the fleece, comb the fibers into the same direction so they can be spun, and spin the fleece onto a bobbin to make a one-ply yarn. With two bobbins full of yarn, I could ply them together to make two-ply yarn—perfect for knitting sweaters. Of course, with three little boys at that point, this didn't mean I had time to knit a sweater, or even mittens—that came later.

After many months of practice and frustration, I managed to become more proficient at spinning. Over the years I've spun flax into linen thread, spun bamboo fiber, and even spun cotton thread from recycled Civil War uniforms. Spinning wool is not season specific, and it doesn't require electricity—you can even spin by candlelight! It fills me with purpose, calm, and a sense of connection to the past, remembering how people have been spinning fibers for centuries. When we welcomed our little flock of sheep, I was able to spin yarn from our own wool! And later, when the llamas came into our lives, we had a ready source of llama wool, too.

Somehow I found that doing all these projects, often more than one at once, helped keep me sane. Doing things like making decorations for the holidays with the children, baking intricate birthday cakes and making fun parties for them, making gourmet dinners for no particular reason, and knitting and sewing dresses for the girls became part of the fabric of our lives. I looked for any reason at all to do fun things. Beyond my enjoyment, this was the best way for me to push out the bad memories—by making new ones. Sometimes, the kids would see me crying after a conversation with my parents, but I tried to keep my sadness from intruding on them. As the years went by, when they met relatives and cousins from my side of the family, they could easily sense the reality and gravity of the situation. For my part, I could see how progressively more angry and empty my mother and sister became. I knew I did not want to become anything like them, and they had caused me to lose too many years of my life already.

As you can imagine, having a family with five children, with the oldest and youngest ones only eight years apart, meant living with a certain level of chaos.

We constantly navigated through a house with toys scattered underfoot, and I struggled to keep track of laundry and shoes, not to mention fast-disappearing supplies of candy. And then there were the animals—our dogs and cats, the chickens, ducks and turkeys, and finally the sheep. Taking care of our "bummer" lamb—a lamb whose mother couldn't care for it—may have been the high, or low point, in our family's inclusiveness, or craziness. "Gorgeous," as Scott named the baby diaper-clad lamb, moved into the house with us, and everyone pitched in, feeding and generally spoiling her till she was old enough to join the other sheep.

As much as we loved where we were living, our house *was* getting pretty overcrowded, and we missed the East Coast and the seasons. When Will was offered a job back east, we decided to move. Preparing to make this big move, we told our children we were going to be like pioneers, and could only bring the things we would need once we got there. It's not a happy thing to have to tell a child, "No, you cannot bring all your Legos," or, "I know you love our ducks, but they are not allowed on a plane even if they *do* fit in a nice little box!" Somehow we all ended up on the plane, without leaving behind any of our kids—our most precious possessions.

We moved into our dream house in Massachusetts—a historic farmhouse with acres of land—and I threw myself into fixing it up and settling in. The things that surrounded us changed. Living with four distinct seasons meant five pairs of shoes, rain boots, and snow boots. As the kids grew older, diapers and cribs became a thing of the distant past, little Lego pieces gave way to skateboards and sleds, and all that candy led to the occasional cavity and trips to the dentist. The early thrills of potty training and big-kid beds were replaced by the thrill of passing a driver's test and buying a first car, and play dates were overshadowed by prom dates.

When I look back at all the things that were part of our lives, it's so clear that none of them matters as much as the experiences they were part of. One object, lost in that big move, forced me to learn that distinction in a personal way. Somewhere in a landfill lies the little glass Bambi my maternal grandmother bought me as a child in Canada. It was my only memento of my kind, generous, artistic grandmother, who gave me the closest thing to a feeling of maternal love I had as a little girl. I cried when I realized that figurine was gone forever. Now, I hold my memories of her and the gift she gave me in the stronghold of my heart. Sometimes the things we let go of (or lose) can leave a wonderful space for more beautiful memories to fill. As our children's lives unfolded, things we possessed faded into the background, while the experiences of even a seemingly uneventful day left us with memories that continue to bring our hearts such happiness. The memory of a magical white blanket of snow covering everything in sight remains vivid, even after the very first snowball the children froze met its demise when they left the freezer open weeks later. In the summertime we savored the delicious peaches and pears we picked in our backyard orchard; even the fruits we canned and jarred for year-round enjoyment are long gone now, but summer always conjures up those memories.

Over time, all these wonderful experiences helped me to untangle the painful knots of my life. But for me, the healing didn't go in a straight line. I continued to harbor the hope that I could somehow prove to my parents and my sister how wonderful my family and I were, as a way to finally win their approval and love. I cried many tears, and endured more vicious cycles of hope and disappointment. But I kept working on myself in therapy, and soaking in the love of my family. Finally, as I came out of the depression that had landed me in the psychiatric treatment program, I was able to end my relationship with my mother, as it had been up to then. She still could not even revisit any aspect of our past. She "couldn't remember" what she had done, or she had "tried her best to be all she could be." Either way, it always came down to a defensive refrain: "You never walked in my shoes." I suffered at my family's hands for too long. I do wish them well, if only because I hope they don't choose to abuse anyone else. Sadly, I see the family cycle continuing with my sister's children. I cannot help them. I can only reach out to others, hopefully through this memoir—and show there *is* hope and survival once you escape beyond the reach of the abusers.

Just outside our house is something that reminds me how crucial it has been for me to learn to nurture myself. Long ago I had dreamed of having a small haven to call my own. When we moved into the house we now live in, I became enchanted by an old tree just outside our breakfast room. I hung round mirrors from the branches, and I would watch them twinkle and sway in the breeze. For me this tree was the closest I could come to the little haven I always wished for. Then this lovely tree began to die. One by one, we had to cut off its branches, and finally the tree had to come down. That day, Jennifer said, "You know, mom, where that favorite tree was looks so sad. I think you should build a cottage there!"

That's how my Lavender Nest Cottage came to be. Eventually, the garden shed that Will had agreed we would build evolved into a perfect, tiny cottage, with windows, a front and back door, a loft, and a back porch. I worked alongside the handyman we had hired, and soon it also had insulation, drywall, a wooden floor, shutters, and window boxes—even electricity, air conditioning, and heat. The front and back doors and all the windows are retired from old homes. I painted the outside walls in shades of lavender and celery, then painted wisteria "growing" next to the front door. Inside, I re-covered a sofa and made curtains in matching English fabric with pale pink cabbage roses.

My Lavender Nest Cottage is now home to my spinning wheel, my art supplies, and my easel. It's a place for me not just to be creative, but also to dream, think, and recharge. This magical place truly nourishes me. In a way it's like a gift to my long-ago child-self, as well as a living symbol—a tangible reminder that I'm safe now, I can take care of myself, and sometimes I can just play when I need to.

After the years of struggle and joy I experienced, I finally let myself realize that *I was still here! I survived!* I was given a husband and children who loved me and only wanted to be loved back; I could do that! Perhaps I *was* worthy! I finally realized what I had missed all along. We are all gifts. We *are* all meant to be here. It was neither my job, nor my purpose, to teach my mother how to love me. It *was* my job to feed that fire burning in my soul, so that I could be everything and more for the six souls who are my universe.

Letting go was a pathway to living. Holding hatred in our hearts takes up room where love could grow. Will, this beautiful, loving man who has given me so much more than I could ever describe in words, was willing to stand by me in the hard times. He supported me in every way as I tried to mend my battered, twisted heart. I could never thank him enough for all that he has done for me and also for our kids and their future families. It is proven that abuse repeats itself. He has helped me to sever that tether.

Although I never intended to be a poster child for anything, my pain will have been well worth it if I can become a source of hope for at least one other person. We were all born to be loved. Sometimes that just doesn't happen; but inside of us there is a spark that can keep our souls alive and warm until we are strong enough to nurture ourselves. When that day finally comes, there is no going back!

After thirty-five incredible years of marriage, and five just-as-incredible children, I can look back and know that happy endings *do* exist! When one candle is used to light another one, its brightness and strength are not diminished. And so, courtesy of the man who *really* wrote this beautiful story, I reach out to you, to ignite your spark. You, too were born to be loved...

NOVEMBER 2010

Autumn greetings to you, our dear friends!

The holidays are fast approaching and 'tis the season to take our familiar place in your mailbox. This year, like all years past, I hold steadfast to my conviction; I'd much rather write a holiday letter than rake leaves. Will doesn't feel the same way. He loves this mundane, insanely tedious, never-ending task—I mean he seems happy to rake the leaves! So, while he rakes leaves, I write this annual holiday letter.

The wonders of this colorful season are so bountiful—leaves lazily catch a ride in the autumn breeze; pumpkins, corn stalks, and bittersweet vines adorn porches and doorways; baskets full of Honeycrisp apples welcome us at farm stands; and I open the front door of our 1830's farmhouse to welcome you into the journey of our family's past year.

This past year's comings and goings were many, thankfully all of them happy ones. It seems our brood is leaving our nest, one by one. Have no pity on us, however; our seemingly "empty nest" is actually becoming our nest of tranquility. Will and I have truly enjoyed the task of raising five children, albeit often waving to one another as we divided our tasks between religious school, sports practices, birthday parties, and back-to-school nights at sometimes as many as four different schools. Now, after 28 years of marriage, we are ready to enjoy each other and sit back in our Adirondack love seat while we watch the kids flourish and pursue their dreams. When they were young, we childproofed the house; somehow now, they still get back in. They know where to find the free food—I mean, they know they are always welcome!

Scott and Pamela, his girlfriend of more than three years, have welcomed Holly, a sweet and spunky Cockapoo, into their lives. Balancing work with play, Scott is nearly finished pursuing his master's degree in information systems at Boston College, and he is now assistant director of web development at Boston College, while continuing to enjoy working at his own web design company. Besides playing in a co-ed softball league with friends, both he and Pamela embrace fitness and work out, whether in the gym or, now, running with Holly!

Robert, our Energizer Bunny, is now living in Brooklyn, where he finally feels at home. He continues working as a freelance media designer and videographer, recently filming for 50 Cent, Estelle, and other clients. On one recent shoot, Lindsay Lohan accosted Robert, thinking he was a paparazzo! Robert and his roommate, Brian, are working together as a media design team, and they enjoy entertaining in their huge apartment. In the coming year, Robert hopes to get back into acting professionally and find a wife. He feels that in order for this to happen, he also needs to get a dog—so women will stop to admire it, giving him a chance to pursue them.

Pursuing a simultaneous B.S. and M.S. in materials engineering at Boston College is twenty-year-old Alexander. Working with freshmen as a teacher's assistant in computer science, he continues to spend his spare time killing virtual dragons, Orcs, and aliens who are hell-bent on destruction, while winning horses and gold. Working on classes from polymers to Greek literature to macroeconomics, Alexander takes it all in stride, meanwhile doing work involving analyzing a web-based data application, updating a team intranet site, and surveying electric meters as part of his work-study program. (If you think I understand any of this, you are simply mistaken!)

Eighteen-year-old Jennifer just began her freshman year at the University of Vermont. When she used to trespass in her siblings' rooms seeking treasures to appropriate, I worried she would someday major in petty theft… Ironically, she is majoring in criminal justice with a minor in social work. Jennifer remains active in causes for which she feels passionate, especially equal rights. She has joined her college rugby team, and in her free time, she enjoys playing guitar and songwriting. Loving college life and the beautiful view of the mountains, she hopes to take full advantage of winter's ample snowfall and engage in one of her favorite activities—snowboarding.

Skyping with her boyfriend in Scotland is seventeen-year-old Nicole's main priority, while emptying the dishwasher and feeding the dogs fit under the category of "I'll do it later." For her room décor, she still seems to prefer the "we've just been robbed and they've emptied every drawer in my room" look. This past summer Nicole got her driver's license; this gave her the perfect opportunity to get a job, which entailed driving an elderly woman on errands and to work each day. Nicole's observations are keen, and she is still the first to offer hugs or advice. Nicole has been visiting colleges on the East Coast. Always waiting for her at home are her three cats, Storie, Paisley, and Timmy, as well as the infamous Winchester and Mabel, the stuffed pigs whom she has loved since birth, although they now lack fur, eyes, and stuffing...

The two furry wonders who own all of our hearts are our female miniature schnauzers, Shadow and Snowball. They are filled with the purest love there is, while their crate is filled with everything they deem to be theirs. As adorable as they are adoring, even their "cousin" Holly finds them irresistible. When she comes to visit, the three of them tear up the house—I mean, frolic like there is no tomorrow!

Home is where I hang my many hats these days! There is no better place to indulge in all that I have been yearning to accomplish since the kids were little. While I continue to love my position as a SANE nurse (Sexual Assault Nurse Examiner) and still paint murals in homes and businesses, I spend a lot of my time in my sweet little Lavender Nest Cottage, doing everything from medical illustration to spinning wool, knitting, and oil painting. This past summer I enjoyed navigating my way through landscaping the front and back yards of the cottage; I built winding stone and brick paths, and I even made a stone wall with lavender plants adorning the edge. This little cottage fulfills my every dream.

Longing to be free from emptied pockets—that is, college tuitions—is Will. He continues to enjoy caring for patients and working with residents and students, as well as writing for both books and journals. Two of Will's research papers were accepted by an international medical society, prompting his invitation to Seoul to present them. This led to our amazing ten-day trip to South Korea, including the gorgeous Jeju Island. While unequivocally dedicated to both his profession and family, this sweet man gives every ounce of his heart to ensure that we are happy and well cared for.

And so, as this holiday letter comes to a close, and we begin our journey into a new year, we'll take this opportunity to wish you a warm and wonderful holiday season, one which overflows with everything and everyone you hold dear. From our nest to yours, HAPPY HOLIDAYS!

Much love,
Will, Dana, Scott, Pamela, Robert, Alexander, Jennifer, Nicole, and the whole menagerie

Epilogue

*Y*ou might wonder how things stand between my mother and myself these days. Long ago, thanks to the work I did in therapy to undo the damage from my childhood—all with Will's unflinching support—I let go of the hatred. I gathered all the toxic debris of my relationship with my mother, and I put it in a box with her name on it. I no longer own the baggage she placed upon me. What a burden was lifted!

Years before, I had written my mother a long letter, in response to her blowing off my invitation to her to visit us, saying she had a dentist appointment. Then I fell into the terrible depression that led to my getting intensive psychiatric help. My mother's response to my letter was predictable; she decided to act as if I didn't exist. But in a new twist, she attempted to replace me with one of our children, reaching out to that child with phone calls and letters. She insisted that although our relationship was irreparable, she saw no reason there would be a problem having a relationship with our children. This almost caused my boat to capsize—how was my relationship with her irreparable when she had made absolutely zero effort to fix it? How could she simply sail on to her next victims, my children? Will and I put an end to this malicious attempt to divide our family.

Now, years later, my mother and I have a neighborly, casual friendship. The "wave and chat over the fence" kind of sharing. It's not ideal, but it's ok. I didn't choose my childhood, but I did choose the type of relationship we will have from here on. It works well because I keep her at a distance and share only safe things with her. I choose to believe that I hold my head high, and keep my self-respect and integrity, because I have been able to find a safe relationship, albeit a superficial one, with her. In reality, she missed out on many years in *my* life.

I could only live with contentment and a humble heart if I believed that she did want to love me, but she chose not to help herself to become that loving mother. And my thoughts are the same for my father: he may have loved me, but he also chose not to help or protect me. These, however, were not my choices, nor were they my responsibility. My responsibility was to break the caustic chain that binds generations one to the other, by giving my children the gift of a childhood that celebrated *them*. I feel I have done that, especially because I went to great lengths to not only eradicate the negative force instilled within me by my mother, but, moreover, become their advocate, loyal supporter, and cheerleader.

As a parent, I can look into her sad, lonely soul and feel compassion for her. I can do this because I chose a path that was not the one she dropped me off at. I made my own trail. Just because you fell off the happy wagon at birth does not mean you must allow it to perpetually run you over! I will admit that our children have a difficult time with my renewed relationship with my mother. Trust me, it is not anything near what I have with my children! As you know by now, I took my childhood experiences and tried to do the opposite with our children. I took my job as mother very seriously.

After all is said and done, when my children are on their own, I'm hopeful that they will remember me as loving and kind. Even when they were little, at each day's end I would take some quiet time, in order to assimilate the day. Did I impart love into their hearts? Did I teach them that it is not what you accomplish in life, but how you impact others that truly counts? Did I teach them to respect others' challenges and reach out to ease them?

I took to heart what our first pediatrician always reminded me, "Talk to your children! Even when they are infants, they can gather information by the tone of your voice. When they are older, there will be good communication because they will know your heart from all the sharing over the years." He was right. I always explained my reasons and my heart to them. They knew where I was coming from, even if they didn't agree.

My parents operated under the guise that they were perfect and not ever to be questioned. This created a disconnect that I could not wrap my mind around. Now, communication is a priority in our family. How can you respect another's feelings when you don't know how they are feeling? We talk, explain, and share often. Our children know that they can call any time of the day or night to tell us anything! We never promised not to be angry, but we will love them no matter what, and will be there for them to help them right any wrong. By the same token, I want our children to know that we are their parents, but we are not perfect, and we never will be! Now, if I find that I am wrong, I admit it immediately and ask my children's forgiveness. As for the inevitable punishments, Will always had a gift for carrying them out in as respectful a way as was possible, so they would learn from their mistakes. He would explain why what they had done was wrong, and then he would ask them to choose their own punishments. And it worked. They always knew where they stood with us; there were no surprises and no misunderstood punishments. I've always told our children that perfection is not human. We are inherently flawed beings! As Teilhard de Chardin said, "We are not human beings having a spiritual experience. We are spiritual beings having a human experience."

When I'm in the middle of a situation, I try to ask myself, what will they remember from this? Will they remember having made the best decision they could at that time in their life, or will they remember Will or me screaming that they were making a ridiculous decision? I *never* want to choose the latter! We always encouraged them to embrace the journey.

Will and I have a beautiful, fulfilling relationship with each other and with our children. One of the things I realize is that I have so much energy and zeal for life because I feel I have *so much* catching up to do. There will always be tons of room in my heart for happy things, because I hang a "No Vacancy" sign for those who do not come from a place of goodness and respect. Even at nighttime and on my darkest days, my flame is flickering away, lighting my trail.

This is the letter I wrote to my mother—the one that set the seeds for our new relationship.

> *Dear Mom,*
>
> *I sit in my favorite little spot, in my kitchen, at my computer, with a magnificent view from the windows that surround me. This is where I wrote our holiday letters over the past thirteen years. My view is even more beautiful this year.*

The view is much the same as every spring; the grass is once again green, the flowers are in bloom, the trees now have leaves. But my view, it is unbelievably different. It is magnificent, in fact. It is filled with more hope than I ever thought possible. I can see for miles into the future I so look forward to. Yes, there are clouds that float by, but I now know what sunshine looks like, and I know it always comes back again. It's kind of like the hope that lived in the corners of my heart when my world seemed so dark. It lit my way.

So many years have passed since I endured the lingering pain I suffered at your hands and words. In looking back, I know that this pain made me who I am today. In a strange way, you are the one who made me the mother and wife that I am. No one else can take so much of the credit. You see, you taught me virtually everything not to be. You showed me what happens to a sweet, tender soul when you belittle it and mash it to a pulp. You showed me what happens to a child when they are told they are not acceptable the way they are, and especially when they do not fit into the molds their siblings fit into. You showed me what happens to a child when they have themselves been abused—and they fail to delve through, and overcome, their pain. You showed me what happens to a soul that never grows beyond that pain and never grows up. It only grows old, never having enjoyed a life well lived. It repels happiness and only attracts others who have suffered a similar existence. I now watch you growing older, colder, and finding no shoulders to cry on, from those you used up. People only have so much they will allow you to take from them. You almost took all of me.

As I journey further into motherhood, as our children leave our nest to explore their own worlds, I feel only compassion for you. No, I cannot forgive you, because in fact, you did take away from me what should have been a promising childhood and early adulthood. Sometimes I think that if I forgave you it might invalidate all that I went through. Maybe it might even suggest that your abuse never really happened. I know it did. But, my journey has led me to find a comfortable relationship with you. You see, you cannot hurt me anymore. While you tore down my soul like ugly wallpaper that the homeowner can't stand to look at, you built one strong woman, just like the walls the wallpaper is hung on! You pushed me further than most souls can, or will, ever go! And for that, I cannot thank you enough.

I can look back and remember that innocent child who only lived for your love. Despite the withholding of your acceptance and affection, you taught me that everyone has love to give, even though they might not know how to release it from a heart under lock and key. When you need what you cannot get, you look elsewhere to find it. I did. I found a husband who loves me more than I will comprehend. He always has loved me. He gives me more happiness than most people can enjoy in an entire lifetime. He has a heart that knows no anger, sadness, or discontent. He lives life to the fullest. I get to walk beside him through life and enjoy every single moment! I was entrusted with five beautiful children to raise.

Yes, God fulfilled His part of our pact. He created these sweet, tender souls who make a difference in their worlds and others' lives. They will never, ever doubt just how much I love them. I am madly in love with my family. The family I almost left—to fend for themselves in the absence of a mother who felt too tormented to go on. When I stepped away from our Washington balcony, I walked into a future that I enjoy beyond belief. I get even more joy when I get to share it with you. You get to see all that you never experienced. You see, tortured, fractured souls never open enough to allow these things in. They only smell the culinary brilliance on the supper table before them, but they cannot taste anything. They see the world around them buzzing past, yet with a scope is so limited that they can only see others as walking away from themselves. I almost walked away from you, my pain, and my life! I delved through the insurmountable pain, to enjoy a life so full of every-thing you missed. Because of that, I offer you empathy, kindness, and the hope that you might actually never truly know the pain you exacted on others. That might offer you more guilt than you could endure. You never found or felt happiness, so why would I wish you pain?

To hate you or hold a grudge would serve no purpose. Not only did I in fact survive and become stronger, but I stopped the pattern you continued. While I cannot allow myself to embrace the fact that you never took steps to heal yourself, thus preventing the abuse you inflicted on me, I can embrace the child you still are. I embrace the fact that you never grew to understand the ways of the world. You never got to truly see me as I evolved from a depressed, pitiful, cracked vessel into a beautiful vase that holds flowers every single day of my life! You missed so much! I cannot help but pity you, while at the same time, wanting to make the last years of your life full of as much joy as you are capable of experiencing. You gave me life, even though you almost took it, too, and I now look to the future to show our children how to understand and find empathy for others' stories. Some people live the same chapter day in and day out. They cannot find a way to write new chapters. They find a painful comfort in holding onto the events and characters of their past. They could not deal with the losses of the only family they ever knew, and they hold on instead to the pain these people left within them.

I choose not to hold on to the pain you gave me. You see, to do that would destroy and prevent all I have become! I would have stopped short and taken a path that would lead me to your destination. More than anything else, what kind of mother would I be? How could I love my children so completely with a heart filled with anger, resentment, and hatred for you? What would I be teaching them were I to live a life filled with only sadness, bitterness, and ignorance that results from holding onto the baggage that used to take my soul from place to place, as I ran from all that you were and were not.

These days my kitchen is always decorated with the accoutrements of the current season. I no longer have to wait for a holiday; every day is a cause for celebration and decorating my soul and those wonderful souls around me! This charming farmhouse kitchen is filled with the amazing smells of cooking and baking. Our children still recall all the times their friends stood by my stove awaiting a taste of my latest creation. I hope they will never forget these times and all the joys we shared as I stood by my stove, as we laughed and shared and enjoyed one another to the fullest.

Things aren't hopping in the Andrews household these days; they are RISING! Will and I have two hundred pounds of grain in our basement; I have two grain mills that I use to grind the wheat for flour I use in making wonderful, healthy loaves of bread. I continue, more than ever, to answer to the call of my need to create whatever my soul deems the project for the day. I am unafraid to endeavor and undertake new projects. That's because of you!

I celebrate you, Mom. Because of you I know not to be afraid, not to give up. You continue to inspire me to become so much more! To live life with a curiosity, and to know that I was born for greatness and to bring joy to any and everyone I can. You inadvertently lit a spark at my birth. I hope that through this book, the spark that began with you will light others' sparks, and they will, in turn, continue to light the sparks of others.

It is my fervent wish that you will embrace this story that I tell. You and I both know it is the truth. I fear that it is not within your capacity to look back and take any responsibility for anything you did, said, or perpetuated. I also know that you tell me how proud you are of me and my family. I hope that you can somehow find the inner peace and solitude we all deserve. I hope you know that I believe you tried your best, and that you were simply unable to climb outside of your own pain, to give me the love and belonging I deserved. More than anything else, I hope that before you journey on as you breathe your last, you will have come to a place that is peaceful and filled with love. Each time we talk on the phone, or in person, I remind myself that you are still a soul craving so much! I try my hardest to give you all the love and empathy I can. No one else ever did.

Lastly, it is with unconditional love that I hold you in my heart. I cannot withhold love from my children and husband, and I certainly would not teach them well if I were to withhold it from you. I want you *to know that I needed to write this book. This is the journey I deserve to celebrate. I invite you to come along with me. You lived in my heart all along. You are welcome to share this magical place I have come to call home. I will always be here to light your spark when you find it. Everyone deserves a light so they can see the beauty in their lives.*

I wish you peace and love, not only at holiday time, but with each new day you awaken to. I wish you a heart, like our hearth, which fills with warmth in winter, and a view like that in my kitchen, where you see the joys of each new season. I wish you compassion from others, too. As much as I wish things in our past were different, I celebrate the fact that we can talk, share, and look forward. I always believed that a future existed for us, one where we could be mother and daughter. Even though I took the role of mother, and you the childlike daughter, I will love you. All souls were created to be loved...

Although this was my last letter to my mother, she will sadly be a part of my life forever. Don't get me wrong. I have no desire or reason to be a part of her life, but the damage she did to my soul will continue to be a daily challenge and hindrance for me. Most days, I mute the nasty names and threats she pounded into me with the white noise of my mind, inwardly repeating, "You are worthy, and your role is not to continue to gain her love or recognition. You have a purpose, and your purpose is to make a difference for others." I do my best to remind myself that she could have helped herself—if she allowed herself to recognize that she had a problem. A huge problem. She only recognized *me* as her problem, and was/is simply incapable of ever taking responsibility for any of her actions.

Sadly, I must share that there is no longer a place left in my life for this woman who robbed from my soul every day. Each time I spoke with her by phone, I was faced with the reality that I was not honoring myself by pretending I cared about her. Will and our children questioned why I'd forfeit my own self-respect on her behalf. I cannot wipe away the evidence of her intrusions. All I can do is remind myself that I *am* supposed to be here, and I have my own family now. On many days, this works. Too often, it fails. She left her mark on me, and I can never wipe it away. I need to remind myself that new pains, like the ones that were opened when I wrote my last letter to my mother, will fade into an occasional dull ache. I share this with you so that you will understand that a wounded soul bears scabs that can still be torn away. The smallest memory or incident can cause the blood to flow. My sweet Will and our children help the wound to close again.

It is unfortunate that the heart remembers even those things I wish it would not. My heart now tries to replace her with others, and I will always try to seek acceptance and validation. You see, she wiped away my internal ability to believe I am inherently good. Just living and breathing doesn't seem enough. My boat floats on an ocean with a tide that changes drastically on any given day. There is no warning of an impending storm. Suddenly on some days, a hurtful incident or small remark will turn the clouds dark. The ocean waves reach record highs, my soul shakes and rocks, and I cannot maintain my footing on the deck. Other days, there is a cloudless sky, the waters are calm, and I feel complete. My family is my life preserver, but they can't calm the howling winds, nor shield me from the storm that makes me feel I'm about to suffocate and drown.

Thankfully, Will and I have given our children more than a tiny, flimsy raft. They each have sturdy vessels, strong enough to weather the damage my mother tried to inflict on them. They understand the gale-force strength of her actions, and they know to avoid them.

Somehow in the final stage of my acceptance and closure, I realized that there was a little more to be said... to my dad. After recently attending the funeral of the father of a close friend, I was struck by the most pronounced differences between his father and mine. The eulogy my friend wrote and shared was both breathtaking and riveting! It captured the life and heart of an uncommon yet common man. He had no education, but he was wiser than most people could ever hope to be. On the way home from his funeral, these words poured out of my soul like raging white waters:

> *Dear Dad,*
>
> *As the writing of this book nears completion, I find myself compelled to write these words to you. I don't imagine letters or emails find their way to heaven, but my words need to get to you somehow, otherwise they will remain forever left unsaid.*

Only several times in our father-daughter relationship did I truly feel a connection to your heart. Oh, how I always wished to have, and will always long for, a chance to be Daddy's girl. I wanted you to praise me, to adore me, and be my greatest fan. I wanted you to sing me a lullaby to chase away my night terrors and hug away my growing pains. I wanted to have my own spade and hoe so we could plant the vegetable garden and reap the harvest together. I wanted you to take me to a father-daughter dance, and dance with joy when my sweet Will asked me to marry him. I wanted you to be there to cry when I found "THE" wedding dress I would wear as you walked me down the aisle. I wanted to rest my weary head on your shoulder when I tried to learn how to be a mother and how to mother myself—because my own mother was a mother in name only.

Yes, there are so many things I wish for, but I'm helpless to ever gain. I will, however, ensure that Will is all these things and more for our girls! (I am the gardener, so I will be the one to share my garden tools and responsibilities with our children!)

Deep within me, I trust that yours was a kind, compassionate, and loving heart. Sadly, like a long string of entangled Christmas lights, you were rendered useless to me because of Mother's needs, which had to take precedence over mine. You had such promise to be colorful, bright, and joyful. Instead, you remained boxed within cellophane, where others could see a soul twisted and knotted in a heap, never to provide true joy or show the colors it was capable of.

I missed out on the best part of you, but finally I can look at beautiful Christmas lights and feel joy! You see, I don't need to forgive you for what I had to forgo; you knew that you made that choice when Mother forced you to choose between us. You knew that I was strong, industrious, tenacious, and WOULD find my way even without your hand to hold. You knew I would fall and fail, but you also knew I would summon the courage to dare to dance even on horribly painful days spent finding my way to loving myself, my husband, and our sweet children.

I cannot bring myself to imagine that there are no windows from heaven; you deserve to see that I AM ok! I grew a set of wings so that if I began to fall, I could fly. I taught myself to plant and reap, in so many ways! Although I could not have the experiences a loving, involved father could provide, I will settle for knowing that with every accomplishment, both small and big, you are with me. I know this book will make you proud. I know we are ok.

If you have shared the same perilous journey I did, or a similar one, do not expect the waves to take responsibility for the damage you suffered. It will most likely never happen. Inasmuch as you have been captive to the sea witch, it is up to you to recognize and repair the damage to your vessel—to build a stronger boat and sail another sea. No one else should suffer your fate or weather the storm you could have saved them from.

There *is* help. There *is* hope. You owe it to yourself to strengthen and nurture yourself. You are worth it, no matter what you were told. No matter what you believe, you are meant to be here, and your healing will allow you to reach out to others who are still within the grasp of hands that threaten to strangle the life from them.

Please take my story into your heart. Please know that there is life beyond the carnage such as I continue to learn to walk away from. There will always be storms at sea, but now I have a stronger boat for myself, the life preservers of my loving family, and the belief that I can continue my journey.

Made in the USA
Lexington, KY
10 January 2018